A Quiet Kind of Catastrophe

CHRISTINA DCOSTA

About the Poet

Christina Dcosta is a poet who writes from the depths of sleepless nights and ink-stained hands.

Living a quiet life within the suburbs of Mumbai, as a third year English Literature student, she searches for poetry in small observations.

Her work 'A Quiet Kind of Catastrophe' captures the messy, beautiful, and often painful journey of human emotion, love, loss, longing, and quiet resilience. With a voice both confessional and poetic, Christina invites readers into the spaces where silence speaks loudest and where healing begins. When not lost in words, she finds solace in solitude, old memories, and the simple moments that linger between breaths.

Published by,

Notion Press

Author: Christina Dcosta

Poetry Collection (English)

This is a work of fiction. Names, characters, places and incidents either are the product of the author's imagination or are used fictitiously. Any resemblance to actual people living/dead/recently divorced, events, or locales is entirely coincidental.

Copyright © 2025 by Christina Dcosta

All rights reserved.

The opinions expressed in this publication are those of the authors and do not necessarily represent the views of the publisher.

ISBN:9798899840265

To those who felt that they never got it right, so they hide their feelings in pages no one would turn.

You're not alone.

Table of Contents

Window Shopping

I wandered the mall like I always do,
not looking for anything, really.
Just trying to feel something
between the smell of roasted almonds
and the shimmer of things I can't afford.
I told myself I didn't need any of it.
But the truth is,
I needed something.

There was this red coat in the window,
cinched at the waist like it could hold me together.
I stood there too long, pretending I wasn't staring,
pretending I didn't want to try it on
just to see what I'd look like
if I were the kind of person
who buys red coats on a Tuesday
without checking their bank balance first.

Sometimes I stop at the bookstore,
run my fingers over titles
like I'm tracing spines I'll never open.
I read the first page of a novel
like I'm borrowing a life.
It's stupid,
how I keep hoping a sentence
might fix something in me.

I watch couples carry bags like trophies,
laughing over iced lattes and matching sneakers.
I smile like I'm in on it too,
but I'm not.
I'm just me.
Just walking.
Just trying not to feel the weight
of everything I can't name.

Once I saw a little girl point at a doll
and her father bought it without asking the price.
I don't know why that broke me.
Maybe because no one ever did that for me.
Maybe because I don't know what it's like
to want something
and be told,yes.

So yeah,
I walk.
I window shop.
I tell myself I'm only looking,
but most of the days,
I'm just trying to see
where I fit
in a world behind glass.

Coffee and You

It begins with steam curling like ghosts from a chipped
ceramic mouth,
the mug is warm in my palms, the silence warmer still.
You tasted like burnt beginnings and sleepless decisions,
dark, bold, unforgiving, an acquired ache.

I sipped you like a dare, lips brave but unsure,
learning the shape of your bitterness without flinching.

You were morning rain behind window panes,present but
out of reach,
always promising softness but leaving me soaked in
cold.

Now I stir honey into the storm,
milk into memory, watch it swirl like clouds softening
the bruise.

Some days, I brew enough for two shadows at the table,
but only mine lingers, stretching long in the quiet sun.

Coffee cools without complaint,
you left with the kind of silence that still scalds.

And yet,
each sip remembers you,
as if the warmth could still bring you back.

The pages of my book

The pages of my book taste like warm, creamy lattes on
a rainy Sunday,
velvet thoughts poured into porcelain paragraphs,
Each sentence is a swirl of cinnamon skies and slow sips
of soul.

The rain outside plays piano on the windowsill,
a lullaby in liquid Morse, spelling stories I already know
by heart.
Clouds wear woolen coats,
and time melts like sugar on the tongue of the afternoon.

My book breathes in my lap like a cat,
soft, alive, and just a little sacred.
The paper smells of roasted dreams and weathered
hopes,
like it's been steeped in a hundred quiet mornings.

Each word is a fireplace flicker,
Each chapter is a woolen blanket I pull tighter around
my bones.
Reality fogs the glass, but in here,
I drink the entire world without lifting the cup.

So let the storm wrap its fingers around the city,
I've found my shelter
in the latte-colored hush
of ink, steam,
and story.

roses wilt with time, like love

Roses wilt with time, like love,
petals that once blushed with promise
now curl inward,
like secrets too heavy to bloom.

The stem holds memory in every thorn,
a soft betrayal dressed in velvet red,
and the scent, oh, the scent,
lingers longer than the flower ever could.

Love, too, begins in full sun,
stretching open with reckless grace,
only to bow slowly beneath
the weight of silence and seasons.

We press roses in books
to keep what time cannot,
but no page can hold
the warmth they once carried.

And love,
pressed too tightly between chapters,
fades just the same,
Beautiful and brittle,
and remembered
only by the ache it leaves behind.

mumma's favorite teddy bear

It wasn't even a bear,
not really,
just a snowman stitched in plush,
with a carrot nose tilted slightly left,
a frayed blue scarf knotted too tight
 like it held all the winters
she never spoke of.

Button eyes, one chipped, one cloudy,
still look at me like they know
what I lost.
What we both did.

Mamma used to keep him on her nightstand,
right next to her tea cup and rosary,
like a quiet guardian
of dreams she never shared.
She'd whisper to him sometimes,
words meant for someone
who wouldn't break
if she cried too hard.

Now he sits in front of her photograph,
still as silence,
draped in dust
and the kind of memories
that only make sense
to the ones who lived them.

No one touches him anymore.
No one asks why he mattered.
But I know.
I know he was the last thing she held
when her hands stopped reaching for this world.

And maybe,
just maybe,
he's still waiting,
stuffed heart stitched with hope,
hoping she'll come back
and tuck him in again.

a father who took roles for two

When morning breaks, the silence fills the room,
Her laughter is gone, now a ghost that lingers still.
He bears the weight of loss, a heavy gloom,
And carries two roles with relentless will.

Both father's strength and mother's gentle hand,
He shields a child who wears her mother's face,
With tender love no one could understand,
He walks the line of grief and saving grace.

Though nights are long and burden pulls him down,
Anxiety and sorrow crowd his mind,
He fights for light where darkness seeks to drown,
A steadfast heart, resilient and kind.

A father who took roles for two, alone,
In love and loss, he builds a guarded home.

ink and silence

I sat in the café,
writing until my pen ran dry,
words spilling out like rain tapping on windows,
soft and endless.

The steam from my cup curled
like a slow sigh,
while the city moved beyond the glass,
a restless blur I didn't try to catch.

My hand kept going,
even when the ink stopped flowing,
like trying to hold onto a fading dream
that slips away just before dawn.

And in that quiet,
when the pen is empty and the page is bare,
I realize the story was never just in the ink,
but in the silence I let myself feel.

beyond life and art

Literature is a bridge,
stretching beyond the pulse of life,
beyond the brushstroke's color,
 beyond the sculptor's stone.

It is the breath between words,
the pause that holds a universe,
Like a quiet storm of thought and feeling,
where human hearts meet across time.

Books are more than simply ink and paper,
they are the soul's mirror and the mind's flight,
a place where joy and grief dance
in the flicker of a candle-lit room,
where voices once silenced
find their way to speak again.

In literature, we live countless lives,
we fall, rise, love, lose, hope, despair,
and still, the pages turn,
carrying us gently through the endless,
beautiful mystery of being.

our eyes are birds with clipped wings

Our eyes are birds with clipped wings,
yearning for skies they cannot reach,
trapped between hope and silence,
fluttering in cages made of unspoken words.

They watch horizons they'll never cross,
longing for flight, for freedom,
but held back by the weight of things
we never dared to say aloud.

An empty tissue box

The box is empty.
I reach for a tissue and find nothing.
It sits there, open and bare,
like the nights I spent crying,
the mornings I woke swollen-eyed,
trying to hold myself together.

Every tissue was gone,
used up by the weight of loss,
by the sound of silence in the house,
by the moments when I thought I might break.

I thought the box would last longer,
like I thought the pain would ease faster.
But grief doesn't care about time or boxes.

Now the empty box just waits,
a reminder of all the tears I've shed,
all the ways I tried to feel less broken.

And still, the grief is here.
Still, the emptiness fills the room,
no tissue to catch the next wave,
no end in sight.

Less of a home, more of a cage

This house isn't a home, it's a cage.
Walls close in like silent guards,
windows show a world I can't touch,
and every door is locked tight by silence.

I pace these rooms like a ghost,
invisible to the ones who live here,
unseen, unheard,
a shadow swallowed by cold walls.

Time drags, heavy and endless,
like house arrest for my heart,
held captive by loneliness,
held hostage by the weight of nothing.

No one loves me here, not really.
Not in the way that sets you free,
only the kind that lets you exist,
but never lets you breathe.

I am lost inside this place,
a prisoner in my own skin,
trapped between four walls,
and the empty space where love should be.

This isn't a home, it's a cage,
and I don't know how to break free.

the couple

I sit beneath the Bandra sky, the evening's glow so pale
A couple clings where rocks meet waves that rage and
break below
Their whispered sighs ride ocean winds, soft songs I
used to know

The sea crashes hard like words once thrown, harsh and
unkind
Their shadows dance in fading light, a fragile, tender
show
And memories ache where love was lost, left scars no
one can find

He wasn't gentle, never kind, a storm that tore my heart
The silence that I begged for, only echoes of his pain
 While they breathe in each other's warmth beneath the
twilight rain

I watch them touch, and wonder if I'll ever find that
grace
Not malice, nor the bitter sting of love's abandoned reign
But gentle hands that heal, and eyes that hold me in their
place

Her laughter blends with crashing waves, so pure, so
free, so true
And I am left with empty arms, with aching wounds, and
pain

Yearning for a love that sees my worth, not shadows to undo

The couple fades into the dusk, their love a quiet flame
While I sit still, remembering what I lost and what remains
A heart that hopes, a soul that waits, for love without the blame.

a token of love to a best friend

It's not in diamonds or silver,
not wrapped in ribbons or placed in glass boxes.
This token I carry for you is quieter,
woven in the small, ordinary moments
we share like secret threads beneath the background
noise.

It's in the way your laughter spills over,
bright and sudden like sunlight through clouds,
and how I can hear the unsaid in your eyes,
a language that's' older than words, deeper than
promises.

You've been my shelter in storms I never named,
the steady hand that reaches when mine trembles,
the voice that speaks softly when the world screams,
a home without walls,
a comfort that doesn't demand but simply gives.

This love between us is not just flashy or loud,
it's also the quiet pulse beneath every conversation,
the patient waiting through distance and silence,
knowing I am not alone when I look at you.

So here, take this token, not wrapped or adorned,
but held in every memory, every heartbeat we've shared,
a love that lives in the spaces between words,
steady and true,
a promise without conditions or need to prove itself.

For you, my best friend,
I offer this,
not just a gift, but a part of me,
a light to hold onto
when days grow dark,
a hand to reach for
when the world forgets how to be kind.

This is my love for you,
not grand, but unshakable,
not loud, but endlessly there,
a quiet forever
in a world that's always changing.

arms like an angel

I didn't expect to feel anything.
It was just another room in the museum,
that kind of cold silence that makes your hands feel
heavier than usual,
where footsteps echo too loud
and everything smells like floor polish and the past.

And then I saw her.

A statue in the middle of the room,
arms outstretched like she had just let go of something
that had taken years to carry,
or maybe she was still trying to hold it, whatever *it* was,
the grief, the hope, the apology that never got answered,
something was hovering there between her fingers
like a goodbye she never agreed to say.

Her face was cracked, not ruined,
there was a kind of softness in the way she leaned
forward,
like someone who has given too much for too long
and is still waiting for someone to notice that she's tired.

I stood there longer than I meant to.
And the longer I looked,
the less she looked like a statue
and the more she looked like a version of me I thought
I'd buried

beneath every year I spent learning how to be quiet
in rooms where I used to be loud.

There was something about the angle of her arms,
like she didn't know whether she was offering something
or bracing for impact,
like she didn't know if she was about to fall
or if she had already fallen and was just too still to
notice.

And in that moment
I didn't care who made her,
or what she was supposed to mean,
because what I saw was a girl
who looked like she'd once believed her softness could
save something,
and now she was trapped in the shape that belief left
behind.

And I knew that feeling.
I had lived in that pose for longer than I realized,
arms wide, voice low, heart on the table like it was a gift
no one really asked for.

No one tells you how much it hurts
to be the one who always reaches first,
how quietly it empties you
when you keep giving and nothing comes back,
how over time your arms don't open as quickly,
and eventually they stop opening at all.

I looked at her the way you look at an old photo
you forgot existed,
the kind that knocks the air out of you
because you didn't realize how much you've changed
until you see the version of yourself who hadn't yet.

And I think,
what broke me wasn't one sharp thing,
it was a thousand soft cuts,
the kind that didn't bleed right away
but kept stinging later,
on quiet days like this one,
when there's nothing left to distract you
from what you used to be.

I wanted to tell her
that I'm sorry.
Not for changing,
but for not saying goodbye properly,
for folding in on myself too soon,
for trading wonder for defense,
for thinking silence was safer than softness.

And maybe what hurt the most
was knowing she'll always stay like that,
arms open, body leaning,
eternally caught in that halfway place
between who she was and what she was trying to
become.

the untouched kettle from my ancestors

It sits there,
half-hidden behind jars of turmeric and dried red chilies,
wrapped in a faded cotton cloth,
its handle worn smooth where fingers once hesitated,
or clung too tightly.

Sunlight slips past the kitchen window,
catching on its dented side,
catching on dust that never quite settles.
It's colder than the morning air,
though the room hums with the scent of cardamom and
wood smoke.

Once, long ago,
the whistle must have broken the silence,
sharp, sudden, like a breath held too long,
like the moment before the sky cracks open with rain.
Now, it waits,
quiet, patient, as if it knows better than to shout.

Sometimes I imagine the hands that lifted it,
the palms pressed against the heat,
steady even when the body was not.
I imagine water bubbling,
rising in slow circles,
the sound of waiting made audible.

No one touches it anymore.
Not because it's broken,
but because it holds too much stillness,
like the pause between words you can't say,
like the space where anger fades into ash.

I wonder what stories it keeps,
the times it held warmth when the nights were cold,
and the times it stayed empty,
just a shape in the dark,
a hollow where hope should have been.

When I look at it,
I don't see metal.
I see the crease of a sigh,
the weight of a name whispered and forgotten,
the tremble in a hand
that never learned to let go.

purple baby flowers and butterfly shaped leaves

The purple flowers are so small, like little drops of color
you almost miss,
nestled in leaves shaped like butterflies,
like they're resting there, tired and soft.

They don't shout or demand attention,
they just sit quietly, like something fragile you want to
protect,
like the kind of thing you'd watch for a while,
and feel your breath slow down.

It's the kind of quiet that doesn't need words,
just the way the light falls on them,
and how they seem almost alive,
even when no one's around.

I'll set myself on fire to keep you warm

I'll set myself on fire,
not with hope, not with light,
but with the desperate ache of knowing you're cold
inside,
that your heart is a winter I can't thaw with words alone,
so I'll burn every fragile piece of myself,
even if the flames claw at my skin,
even if the smoke blinds me and chokes my breath,
because your warmth feels worth every scar I carry,
every ash I leave behind like forgotten memories
scattered in the wind.

You don't see the fire I carry for you,
the silent inferno I try to hide beneath smiles and quiet
nights,
how it spreads through my veins, relentless and fierce,
how it consumes all I am until I'm raw and bleeding,
but still, I stand here, willing to burn in your cold
shadows,
because the thought of you shivering in the dark
breaks something inside me that I can't fix with anything
but this fire.

I am a pyre built from all my broken pieces,
a blaze that threatens to undo me,

and I keep feeding it, burning for you,
even when it feels like I'm losing myself in the heat,
because love, real love, sometimes demands this
sacrifice,
this unspoken promise that I'll destroy myself quietly
 if it means you won't freeze alone.

But hear me,
this fire is not without its pain,
it's not a gentle warmth that comforts,
it's a scorching flame that scars,
that leaves me trembling in the silence after the burn,
when the world has moved on and only the echo of my
sacrifice remains.

Still, I'll burn,
because I can't bear to watch you shiver,
because your cold has become my wildfire,
because in this madness, this breaking, this burning,
I find a twisted kind of love,
a love fierce enough to set me on fire,
again and again,
until I am nothing but smoke
and you are finally warm.

Goodbyes are bittersweet

Goodbyes are bittersweet,
a fragile kiss pressed into the phone,
the last glimpse of you before the screen goes dark,
a whisper caught between cities,
between time zones, between heartbeats.

I hold onto the memory of your voice,
soft and distant like a song fading on the edge of dawn,
while miles stretch wide like oceans
that neither of us can cross tonight.

It's the ache of knowing you're there,
somewhere beneath the same sky,
but out of reach,
a hand I can't hold, a breath I can't catch,
a warmth that feels like a dream I'm afraid to touch.

We say goodbye with promises tangled in longing,
with "I miss you" swallowed in silence,
with "See you soon" that stretches into months,
and still, we carry the weight of that parting
in the hollow spaces where your presence should be.

But goodbyes are not just endings,
they are the tender pause, the quiet hope,
the soft pulse of love surviving distance,
the promise that, somehow, someday,
we'll erase these miles,

and turn these goodbyes
into hellos that don't have to wait.

your tears taste like sugar

Your tears don't taste like salt,
they taste like sugar,
strange and unexpected,
a sweetness that lingers on my tongue
like memories I can't quite forget.

They fall like gentle rain,
not stinging but soft,
carrying a sorrow folded into something tender,
the ache of love that still clings
even when it hurts to hold on.

Your tears are a secret gift,
a sweetness wrapped in sadness,
reminding me that even in pain,
there's a flavor worth savoring,
a sweetness that speaks of hope,
of love that refuses to dissolve.

Sunset at Marine Drive

Marine Drive isn't just a road that curves by the sea, it's
a rib cage that holds Mumbai's beating, stubborn heart.
The pavement cracks under a thousand stories,
spilled like chai on worn concrete,
and you can feel the city breathing here,
fast and full, like someone who doesn't know how to
slow down.

People pour in, strangers who lean into the sea breeze,
lovers who forget the world between held hands,
old men in white shirts and time-stained smiles,
hawkers balancing bags of roasted peanuts and candied
promises,
children chasing pigeons like dreams not yet tired.

Vehicles blur in a slow-motion chaos,
rickshaws, taxis, bikes, honks layered like a discordant
symphony,
each horn a language, a fight, a love letter to urgency,
and the traffic lights blink like tired eyes trying to stay
awake.

In the background, the skyline holds up the sky with one
exhausted hand,
as glass towers reflect the dying light like mouths full of
secrets,
and somewhere in the distance, a train screams past,
a reminder that even the city's veins run restless.

The Arabian Sea crashes gently today,
as if it's making peace with the madness,
its waves dragging themselves back like they forgot
something,
a name, a home, a face.

And as the sun folds into the horizon like an apology,
the world begins to blur, faces, headlights, the boundary
between sky and sea,
but Marine Drive remains,
a stitched hem between land and longing,
between people who have nowhere else to go
and people who come here just to remember why they
stayed.

Mumbai doesn't pause.
It leans against the sea, tired but breathing,
and for a second, so do I.

Lunch at Candies without you.

Candies still sits like an old soul in the heart of Bandra,
tucked between winding lanes, bougainvillea spilling
like secrets
over chipped pastel walls and rusted gates that groan
open
into a place that feels more like a memory than a café.

 I walk past the vintage scooters and old mango trees,
up the faded pink steps that creak like they know our
weight,
where the afternoon light filters through stained glass
in quiet kaleidoscopes, soft, broken things that dance on
the floor.

You're not here, but your absence holds a chair beside
me,
as I sit alone at the corner table near the wall of framed
postcards,
where we stared at each other on our first date and spoke
about the 'what now'
About what we wanted to do, what we wanted to share,
about moving in, about roaming the world,
but never did.

The smell of roast chicken and old wood still lingers,
sweetened by fresh pastries and college kids sharing
fries,
their knees brushing under the table like something
sacred,

and I remember your hand, how it used to find mine
without ever needing to look.

We held hands here, remember?
Right after the coffee, just before the tart,
your fingers trembling slightly, mine anxiously building
sweat
It wasn't perfect, but it was real,
and now, all I have is the taste of sugar
clinging to a spoon that no longer stirs for two.

The restrooms still carry the collage of couple photos,
their grins frozen, love suspended mid-laugh,
and I search their faces for some ghost of us, as if time
had accidentally archived our joy.
But we're not there.
Just whispers in the mosaic tiles,
echoes in the clink of plates
 and the barista's bored hum.

Bandra hums outside like it always has,
rickshaws zipping down Hill Road,
the sea breeze threading through chapel bells,
vendors selling knockoff sunglasses near Lucky's,
and lovers walking slowly, like they have all the time in
the world.

But inside Candies, the air still smells of old love.
Of butter and betrayal.
Of mango juice and the silence we slipped into
before we even said goodbye.

People come here, fall in love,
share forks and playlists and dreams,
and leave with hearts either full or slightly cracked.
We were no different.
Except we never really left.

Even without you,
your laugh, your touch, your half-sipped latte,
this café still holds the shape of us,
still folds us into the corners
like a love letter no one ever posted,
waiting, quietly,
to be read again.

to the crush I couldn't bring myself to confess.

Dear You,

You won't even know this letter exists,
just like you never knew
how much of my life you quietly held
 in the soft curve of your smile.

It began in a tuition class ,
a dingy room with peeling paint and chalk-dust air,
where I first saw you and the world stopped
like it owed me that one moment.
You were just a boy scribbling notes,
and I was just a girl who forgot how to breathe.
It was love at first sight,
the kind that feels foolish in stories
but was scripture in my heart.

And I kept it quiet.
Not out of shame, never shame,
but out of the fear that if I spoke it aloud,
it would disappear.

Over the years, I collected your glances
like seashells from a distant shore.
Our eye contact was never fleeting,
it was electric, something cosmic,
like two stars winking across galaxies,

too far to touch, too close to forget.
I think you knew.
At least a part of me always hoped you did.

You championed my words like no one else did.
"You're going to be something big one day,"
you once said,
and I repeated that line in my mind
whenever I thought of giving up.
You read my poems like they were gospel,
listened to my rants with your chin in your palm,
like time bent just to make space for me
in your busy little world.

And then,
you left.
Shifted to Delhi for your studies,
as if life had decided I had loved enough for a lifetime.
No goodbyes. No messages.
No birthdays exchanged,
no random 'Hey, how have you been's.
Just space. Just silence.
Just the kind of absence that doesn't echo,
it swallows.

For ten years, I kept loving you in secret.
Wrote over 500 letters that never reached you,
buried your name in metaphors and hidden initials,
and every time you came back,
even briefly, even in photographs,
my heart made a fool of itself
all over again.

You don't know how stupidly,
how entirely
I kept falling.
How I compared every "he"
to the dream you accidentally became.
And no one lived up,
because how could they,
when you were everything
I never even had?

It's funny,
how a person can be both
the happiest thought
and the saddest ache.
How you can be the love of my life
without ever being mine at all.

Maybe if I had told you,
maybe if I had looked you in the eye
and said, "It's you. It's always been you,"
things would have been different.
But I didn't.
I couldn't.
And now I don't know
if I ever will.

You're probably out there,
laughing, thriving, loving someone else,
while I'm here,
still writing poems with your name
stitched quietly between the lines,

still waiting for a version of life
where you look at me like I'm not invisible.

But this is the closest I'll ever come to telling you.
So here it is, my confession,
wrapped in too-late and not-enough:

I loved you.
I still do.
And maybe that love will never die,
only grow dustier in the attic of my chest,
where your memory still lives,
 untouched,
 unclaimed,
 forever unspoken.

 Yours never,
 but always,
 Me.

You never came home

I kept the porch light on for months,
like a lighthouse in a storm you never returned from.
Your shoes stayed by the door, untouched,
like they knew better than to walk into a world
that no longer held your warmth.

Dinner got cold every evening,
and I still made enough for two.
The plate beside mine stayed empty,
but I filled the silence with stories
you used to love,
as if words could resurrect you.

I watered your plants.
I dusted your books.
I folded the sweater you left on the armchair,
and it still smelled like your skin,
a scent the wind tried to steal,
but I fought to keep.

The neighbors asked less with time.
First it was "When will he be back?"
then it was silence,
the kind that wraps around your spine
and teaches you how to ache in secret.

I wrote you letters I never sent,
letters with trembling hands and smeared ink.
They sit in a box now,

like relics of a time
when hope still dared to bloom.

You never came home.
But I still hear the creak of the gate
like a heartbeat.
Still look up at every car engine that hums past.
Still sleep on my side of the bed
 just in case.

They say time heals.
But what does time know
of a door that never opened again,
of a hug left midair,
of a last goodbye that never said its name?

You never came home.
And still,
this house is waiting.
And so am I.

To the dress I purchased, but never wore

You hang in the back of my closet
like a secret I never told,
still wrapped in tissue,
creases folded like unshed tears,
tags dangling like unfinished sentences
that never found their voice.

I bought you with trembling fingers
and a heart full of hope.
You were meant for a night
that never arrived,
for laughter under fairy lights,
for dancing when the world finally made sense.

You were supposed to be worn
on the evening he said he'd come,
when he promised,
"I'll take you somewhere special."
And I believed him,
because when you're in love,
even lies wear perfume.

I imagined how you'd feel on my skin,
soft, flattering,
a little bold,
maybe enough to make him look twice

and mean it.
Maybe enough to make him stay.

But he didn't.
He never called.
Never asked what shade of blue
I had chosen to wear for him.
Never knew the dress was you,
my way of saying *I was ready*.
That I was waiting.
That I wanted to be seen.

Now you hang
among other quiet things:
a dusty pair of heels,
a clutch still smelling of lavender,
a version of me that almost was.

And some nights,
I still pull you out,
hold you against me like a memory,
not of him,
but of the girl I was before the silence,
before the unanswered texts,
before I learned that sometimes
you can be beautiful, prepared,
and still,
unchosen.

I keep you,
not because I think he'll ever come back,
but because you remind me

of the girl who once believed
in magic stitched into fabric,
 and love that would see her
if only she shone bright enough.

Tea and Cigarettes

I never smoked until I met you.
You said cigarettes calms your nerves,
that the world felt less sharp when you exhaled.
I didn't understand it then,
but I watched the way your fingers curled around the lighter
like they were made for flame,
the way you blew smoke like secrets
you didn't want to say aloud.

I made tea like rituals,
the kind my mother passed down,
cardamom, ginger, a touch of honey.
You never liked it sweet,
but you drank it anyway
because it reminded you of me.

Our nights were a haze of burnt edges
and porcelain cups.
You, lighting one cigarette after the other,
me refilling the kettle like a prayer,
as if boiling water could wash away
what we were too tired to fix.

We rarely talked after midnight.
Just sat in the quiet,
wrapped in the ache of what we used to be,
the smell of tobacco clinging to the curtains,
my hands around tea too hot to hold,

your eyes elsewhere.
Always elsewhere.

Sometimes I wonder if you loved the smoke
more than the silence I gave you.
If it was easier to burn slowly
than to face what was unraveling between us.
I stayed,
because leaving felt crueler
than fading.

When you left,
you took your lighter,
your ashtray,
your silence.

But you forgot the mug you always used,
the one with the chipped rim,
the one I never washed
because it still smelled like you,
of Marlboro Gold and a love too tired to last.

Now I drink my tea alone.
No sugar.
No honey.
Just bitterness,
and an empty balcony
where the wind doesn't carry smoke anymore,
only the memory
of someone
who once made me feel like warmth and ash
 could coexist.

Tangerines

Tangerines in morning light,
Peeling joy in a quiet bite.
Citrus sun on fingertips,
Golden juice and parted lips.

Sweet and sharp, a memory gleams,
Of laughter lost in summer dreams.
Gone too fast, like all good things,
Love, youth, and tangerines.

Painted in bruises

I am painted with bruises
in places you cannot see,
where silence strikes louder
than fists ever could be.

Where smiles are stitched
with trembling thread,
and laughter echoes
the words I never said.

You look for wounds
on the surface of skin,
but pain is clever,
it hides deep within.

I carry battles
like whispers in my chest,
each heartbeat a reminder
that I never quite rest.

Don't ask me
why I flinch at light,
some days, even hope
feels too bright.

My ribs are galleries
of invisible art,
each shade a story
that shattered my heart.

But still I stand,
a canvas unspoken, fragile and fierce,
beautifully broken.

Forgive me for not being whole

Forgive me for not being whole.
For the spaces inside me where light struggles to settle,
where shadows stretch longer than the day,
and quietness feels less like peace and more like
absence.

There are parts of me I keep folded beneath the surface,
fragile shards of memory and pain I don't speak of
aloud,
not because I want to hide,
but because some wounds are too raw to share.

I carry the weight of things I cannot name,
invisible bruises painted across my bones,
reminders of battles I fought alone
in rooms no one knows exist.

Sometimes I am fractured,
a mosaic of broken edges that don't quite fit together.
I am worn, not by weakness,
but by the relentless pulling of hope and fear,
tangled and fighting inside me.

I don't ask you to fix me or to understand every silence,
only to accept that I am still learning how to breathe
in a world that expects completeness.

Forgive me if I falter,
if I hesitate to trust,

if the parts of me that feel broken
sometimes overshadow the parts that are healing.

I am not whole,
but I am here, still trying,
still reaching toward light in the places that hurt most.

Planting joy in dead soil

Oh, how clever of me,
to keep planting joy in dead soil,
like I'm some gardener of miracles,
watering dust with hopeful tears.

I spread my seeds of happiness,
because that's exactly what barren ground demands,
a little optimism to remind it
It's failing spectacularly.

The soil laughs at me,
dry and cracked, mocking my persistence,
as if it's waiting for me to finally quit,
but no, I keep shoveling dreams into the void.

Maybe someday,
just maybe, the dirt will get bored and decide to sprout
something useful,
or maybe I'm just training for disappointment.

I keep planting joy,
because why not?
If the ground's already dead,
What's the worst that could happen?

Chocolate-stained cups

We sit with chocolate-stained cups in hand,
warm reminders of moments we planned.
Sweetness that melts but leaves its mark,
like silent truths hiding in the dark.

You speak of a love that's flawless and bright,
a perfect tale spun in morning light.
I smile, pretending I fully believe,
while tracing the stains that never leave.

These cups tell a story no words reveal,
of spills and cracks we try to conceal.
Perfection's a dream we both pretend,
but even the sweetest must someday end.

So we sip from vessels worn and flawed,
holding on tight, despite being flawed.
Chocolate rings that won't come clean,
like all the things left unseen, between.

I keep dreaming of doors I've already closed

I keep dreaming of doors I've already closed,
their hinges creaking softly in the night,
echoes of choices locked away,
silent invitations I no longer answer.

In sleep, I wander hallways I left behind,
fingers brushing against frames I sealed shut,
wondering what might have slipped through the cracks,
what voices still whisper from rooms long emptied.

The past is a shadow I cannot shake,
a ghost house built from could-have-beens,
each closed door a portal to what was,
and what will never be again.

Sometimes the weight of those shut thresholds
feels heavier than the walls around me,
reminders that moving forward
doesn't mean forgetting the doors we left behind.

I wake with the taste of old keys in my mouth,
the faint scent of places I once called home,
haunted by dreams of doors I've already closed,
and the restless heart that still tries to open them.

I love you, I'm sorry

I love you.
And I'm sorry.

Not because loving you was a choice I made easily,
but because I can't help it.
It's a force inside me,
a tide that pulls and never lets go,
no matter how fiercely I try to swim away.

I'm sorry for the weight this love places on us,
for the moments it's messy,
for the times it's confusing,
for the way it comes crashing in
when we least expect it,
when we're not ready.

I didn't want to fall like this,
so completely, so blindly,
but here I am,
trapped in the gravity of you,
unable to resist even if I wanted to.

I love you with all the reckless parts of me,
the parts I try to hide or tame.
I love you in spite of the fear that follows,
the vulnerability that shakes my bones,
the silence that sometimes feels louder than words.

And I'm sorry
because I know this love isn't always easy to carry,
it's wild and untamed,
sometimes too much,
sometimes too little,
never quite what the world expects.

But I can't undo it.
I can't unlove you,
even if I tried.

So I'm sorry for loving you this way,
with a heart that breaks and mends a thousand times,
with hands that reach out even when they tremble,
with a soul that aches and sings in the same breath.

I love you. I'm sorry.

Two truths tangled together,
one I can't live without,
the other I wish I could take back.

But this is me,
falling and failing and loving all at once,
hoping somehow you'll understand
that sometimes love isn't a choice,
it's the only thing that feels real.

Parenthesis

Between the lines, (where words don't quite belong,)
I hide the half-truths, the soft sighs, the silent songs.
Not part of the main story, (just whispered aside,)
little secrets that live in the spaces we hide.

They cradle the doubts, (the thoughts we won't say,)
the pauses in conversations that drift away.
A quiet refuge, (a breath held too long,)
where feelings slip softly but never quite wrong.

Parenthesis,
a shadow in the sentence,
a whisper in the noise,
the pause that holds
what's too fragile for the light,
and too loud to be silent.

We build these brackets
around our fears, our hopes,
the unspoken parts of us
that doesn't fit the scope.

But sometimes the parenthesis
is the heart of the line,
the place where truth lingers,
between the curves of time.

Kisses and Hookups

Fingers trace the edges of a fading night,
lips collide in flames that burn too bright,
a hunger sparked in whispered breaths,
a fever rising beneath tangled sheets.

The taste of you, salt and heat and want,
a reckless promise caught on the tongue.
Bodies curve and fold, a language raw,
speaking truths no words ever saw.

Kisses, like fireflies, flicker and dart,
brief sparks igniting the dark.
No names, no futures, just the ache,
a moment's surrender, a daring escape.

Skin pressed to skin, a silent plea,
hooked in the thrall of what cannot be.
We fall into the night's embrace,
lost in the fever of touch and taste.

And when the dawn steals the heat away,
we part like shadows, no words to say,
just the memory of lips on lips,
and the sting of those stolen, endless kisses.

~~I love you~~ I like you

~~I love you~~

 no, not that,
I like you.

Because that's safer, isn't it?
Less weight to carry, less risk to fall.
But we kissed like it was forever,
fingers tangled like secrets no one should know,
and for a moment,
we were everything and nothing,
friends and something more,
lovers for just a breath,
then strangers again.

You yelled at me once,
angry words slicing the quiet,
confessions thrown like punches,
"I'm not ready," you said,
"I don't want to lose you."

And I,
I was furious too,
mad at the silence between us,
mad at the way my heart broke in slow motion
when you pulled away.

But then,
we apologized,

soft words falling like rain on broken glass,
mending the edges just enough to touch again,
to laugh again,
to be friends again.

Because maybe love
is not always fireworks and forever.
Maybe sometimes it's the kiss that almost was,
the anger that almost broke us,
the apology that saved us,
and the quiet knowing
that for now,
this is enough.

 I like you.
And maybe that's the hardest truth of all.

Where do broken hearts go?

Where do broken hearts go
when they don't want to be found?
Not lost in some poetic place,
but hiding under the bed covers,
in the middle of a crowded room,
in the spaces you pretend don't exist.

They don't just heal, do they?
They limp,
they ache,
they curl up in the silence between texts you never sent,
in the ghost of a voice you can't forget.

Sometimes they go to the fridge at 2 AM,
to the same old playlist that feels like you,
broken, raw, searching for answers
that never quite comes.

They sit on the edge of your coffee cup,
in the half-finished conversations,
in the regret that's too stubborn to fade.

Where do broken hearts go?
They go wherever we try not to look,
in the cracks of our smiles,
in the quiet moments before sleep,
and sometimes,
sometimes,
they just stay there,

waiting for someone to notice
and maybe,
just maybe,
hold them close enough to try again.

Save me a part of you when I am gone

When I am gone,
not just from your sight,
but from the rhythm of your days,
from the stories you tell yourself at night,

Save me a part of you.

Save the corner of your smile
where my laughter once lived,
the quiet space in your mind where my voice still
lingers softly.

Hold onto the fragments that don't make sense without
me,
the memories that ache like a song you can't quite
forget.

Save me a part of you,
not to weigh you down,
but to carry me gently,
like a secret whispered only between us.

So when the world feels empty,
when time erases all the rest, there's still a piece of me
waiting patiently in you,
Alive, unforgotten,
home.

trading venom for vigour

I swallowed poison in velvet nights,
each drop a bitter kiss upon my tongue,
venom coursing through my veins,
a silent curse I claimed as mine.

But in the depths of shadowed hollow,
where darkness breathes and secrets bleed, I traded
venom for vigour,
a savage bloom beneath the blackened sky.

The poison burned, then sparked a fire,
igniting cold bones with fierce desire,
not salvation, no, but raw rebirth, a twisted grace carved
from the earth.

I wear my scars like ancient ink,
tattooed in shadows, whispered in blood,
trading venom for vigour,
dancing on the edge of night's dark flood.

No light to save me, no dawn to heal,
only the hunger I choose to feel,
a pulse that drums beneath the gore,
alive in the darkness, forevermore.

Pockets full of love apples

Sunlight spills like honey, warm and slow,
we walk barefoot on cracked sidewalks,
pockets full of love apples,
small, red treasures bursting with summer's promise.

The sticky juice drips down our fingers,
sweet and tart, like stolen kisses beneath the shade of old
maples.
Laughter bubbles up, bright and careless,
as cicadas sing their endless song above.

We carry the taste of long afternoons,
the soft hum of bees, the scent of grass and freedom.
Each bite a memory, each apple a heartbeat,
pockets full of summer, pockets full of you.

Even when the sun dips low and shadows stretch,
the sweetness lingers,
and in those pockets,
love ripens quietly,
ready for tomorrow's warm embrace.

Craving Retribution

Beneath my skin, a fire grows,
a wrath that only vengeance knows.
No peace to calm, no light to guide,
just shadows where my fury hides.

I walk through nights of shattered trust,
where promises decay to dust.
The heartbeat pounding in my chest,
demands that justice be expressed.

I crave the scales to tip and fall,
to see their empire lose it all.
No mercy in this burning plea,
retribution's hunger feeds me.

A storm that rages, wild and deep,
a restless wound that will not sleep.
Until the world pays back its due,
this thirst for vengeance will burn through.

A museum for my love life

If my love life had a museum,
it wouldn't be full of trophies or happy memories.
It would be glass cases holding mistakes,
broken promises, moments I wish I could take back.

There'd be shelves with letters I never sent,
words I was too scared to say,
and pictures of people who meant something once,
now just memories collecting dust.

Rooms filled with kisses that didn't last,
conversations that ended too soon,
and all the times I gave more than I got.

Visitors might walk through and feel the heaviness,
how much I wanted to believe,
how many times I got hurt anyway.

And maybe somewhere in that museum,
there's still a space waiting,
empty but hopeful,
for something real to fill it.

Claw clips and Diet Coke

Claw clips hold back my tangled hair,
while I stare at a screen that won't blink,
alone in a house heavy with echoes,
old memories crowd the corners,
 whispering stories I try to forget.

Empty cans of Diet Coke line the desk,
temporary friends in a silent room,
their fizz long gone but their cold comfort stays,
a bitter taste I can't quite swallow.

I work alone,
no one to share the tired sighs or the small wins,
just the hum of the computer and the clock,
counting down hours that feel like years.

The walls remember laughter that's faded,
pictures on shelves smile like ghosts,
and I'm here, holding onto claw clips and cans,
trying not to feel too lonely,
trying not to feel too much at all.

Between the serpent and the rope

I stand between the serpent and the rope,
two threads twisted with threat and hope.
The serpent coils with whispered lies,
its venom slick beneath calm eyes.

The rope hangs heavy, cold and still,
a silent promise of bitter will.
One bites with poison, slow and deep,
the other waits to pull me steep.

Between the hiss and tightening grip,
I wrestle shadows on my lip,
to choose the pain that burns or binds, or break the
silence in my mind.

No easy path, no gentle way,
just edges sharp where choices sway,
between the serpent's deadly art,
and rope that pulls apart the heart.

So close yet so far

I am a moth circling your fragile flame,
drawn by the heat I both crave and fear.
Each time I edge closer,
my wings catch fire,
scorched by the very light I seek.
I want to land, to rest in your warmth,
but I am always pulled back
by a silent warning I can't name.

You are the shore in my restless sea,
the place I reach for through the tide's endless push,
close enough to feel the salt on my skin,
yet far enough that the waves
swallow me before I can hold you.
I confess:
I am drowning in this space between us,
caught in a current that pulls me away
just as I am about to grasp your hand.

It's this stretch of air,
thick with words we never said,
with fears we buried deep beneath the surface,
that suffocates me most.
I wear my longing like a second skin,
heavy and raw,
an ache that echoes in empty rooms
when your shadow fades with the light.

So close,
that your breath is a whisper on my cheek.
So far,
that distance carves canyons through my soul.

I am caught here,
between hope and silence,
between reaching and letting go,
a fragile heart that can't decide
if it's ready to fall or to fly away.

Eleven years of silent rain

I built you up in my mind,
a storm gathering in silent skies,
each thunderclap a heartbeat,
each flash of lightning a prayer ,
that you might finally see me,
not as a shadow flickering in the dark,
but as a fierce, unyielding light.

I gave you the highest place,
raised you like a towering cloud,
your name a rumble on my lips,
a secret hymn carried on the wind,
held you in the eye of my storm,
where no one else could reach,
where my quiet devotion raged unseen.

But you never looked up.
You never noticed the gathering tempest inside me,
the weight of years held back like rain,
the endless tears trapped in my tear ducts,
waiting eleven long years to pour out
 and drench the world I built for you.

I was a river swelling with storms,
flowing fierce and relentless toward you,
only to crash against dry land ,
a barren place where your eyes should have been,
an empty sky where no lightning struck.

And now I stand here,
bare, unraveling like a sky split open,
the thunder rolling heavy in my chest,
wondering how I mistook absence for presence,
how I worshipped a ghost,
a phantom wrapped in thunderclaps
that never heard the altar I raised.

The pedestal was mine to build,
a fragile cage of storm clouds and hope,
cracking under the weight of truth ,
that sometimes, the love we hold
is nothing but a passing storm,
a story told in lightning flashes,
gone before the rain can fall.

I am left with the echo,
the ache of unshared storms,
and the slow, painful knowing
that to love someone
who never loves you back
is to wait for rain in a drought,
to chase lightning that never strikes,
to drown in tears
that were caught too long
in a storm that should have
broken years ago.

still falling, still unfinished

I keep falling without ever knowing if i want to catch
myself or disappear completely,
holding onto a feeling that is already slipping through
my fingers like something too fragile to keep.
there's this weight in my chest that doesn't let me
breathe, but i'm still here,
still wanting, still breaking, still waiting for the moment
when I'll finally let go or finally stay.

You're in my thoughts more than you should be,
not because i think you're the answer but because i can't
seem to stop asking the question,
the question that has no clear reply and no safe way out,
and I'm tangled in the spaces between wanting you and
needing to walk away.

I don't know how i got here or why I'm still standing in
this place that hurts more than it heals,
where every touch is a risk and every word feels like it
could undo what little peace I have left.
I'm trying to be strong, but the truth is i'm scared ,
scared of what happens if i stop falling,
If I stop believing in the danger that keeps me alive in a
way nothing else can.

there is no ending yet, no closure waiting for me at the
edge of this,
only the unfinished pieces of a story i'm still writing,
and maybe that's the only thing i'm sure of ,

that loving you dangerously means i'm still here, still broken, still trying.

Constellations of dreams

she didn't sleep that night,
not because of some dramatic heartbreak or the chaos of
unfinished deadlines,
but simply because she was bored
and the quiet was louder than usual, and her manuscript
had stopped speaking to her hours ago,
the characters flatlining, the plot as dry as her inbox,
and even the blinking cursor had started to feel like it
was mocking her,
like, really? this again? you think anyone cares about
this girl you're trying to write?
because even you don't.

so she sat there, barefoot, half-curled on the couch,
in the kind of silence that feels like it's pressing its
fingers against your ribs
just to remind you that you're alone.
and then,
almost too perfectly,
it started to rain.

the kind of rain that doesn't ask politely to come in.
the kind that bursts through the sky like it's had enough
of holding back,
accompanied by thunder so loud it sounded like god was
dragging furniture across the floor above,
and lightning that kept illuminating her living room in
short, brutal flashes,

as if the universe was playing photographer for a girl it
had long forgotten to love.

and it should've been annoying,
but instead she watched it,
the storm outside her window,
the wind slapping against the glass like it wanted in,
like it too was sick of being alone,
and suddenly she felt it,
that stupid, romantic part of her that refused to die
quietly.

because she ached for romance
the way some people ache for sunlight after too many
winters.
because romance had always been her favorite
hallucination,
her long-term imaginary friend,
a lover that only lived in her chest,
never in her bed.

and still, she let herself imagine.

because what else do you do at 2:47 a.m.
when the world outside is drenched and dramatic, and
your life inside is neither?

she imagined him,
the boy she once liked too much and told too little,
the one who smelled like cinnamon and recklessness,
the one she never really knew, but loved like she had.

she imagined them running into the street,
laughing like children who had never been rejected,
dancing in puddles that soaked their jeans
and spinning each other under the tall apartment building
like they didn't care who was watching,
like this wasn't something she had made up in her head
to make the night feel less heavy.

she imagined his hands in hers,
the way he'd probably be too tall,
the way she'd probably trip and he'd catch her,
and the way some old Hindi love song would play in the
background,
from someone's open window,
like life had decided to give her one perfect scene,
just one.

and God, for a second,
it felt real,
the weight of his touch,
the water sliding down her spine,
the safety in being seen.

until, of course, it didn't.

until the lightning stopped showing off,
and the thunder grew tired,
and the street below stayed empty.

and she was just a girl again,
alone in her living room,
in the stale blue glow of her screen,

with nothing but caffeine, half-sent drafts,
and a heart full of constellations.

because no one tells you this,
but sometimes love doesn't leave scars,
sometimes it just never arrives.
sometimes it only lives in the quietest corners of your
imagination,
where you name the stars after people who never looked
at you twice,

and build galaxies out of glances,
and call it enough.

because it has to be.

because some girls don't get love stories.
some girls just get
dreams.
and the ache they leave behind.

They say, "Youth is the best years of your life."

They say youth is the best years of your life
but no one tells you that most of it feels like waiting in a
room where nothing really starts,
where your friends fall in love and get kissed in
moonlight
while you scroll past strangers online holding hands with
the life you thought you'd have by now.

they say these are the golden days,
but mine feel like rust ,
like overthinking every text you send and still being left
on read,
like laughing at parties you didn't want to be at,
like collecting memories you're too tired to remember
properly.

they say youth is for wild hearts and impulsive love,
but I have a quiet kind of heart,
the kind that loves too carefully,
falls too softly,
and keeps getting called dramatic
for feeling everything like a flood.

they say this is the time to make mistakes,
but what if all mine just feel like proof

that I'm always ten steps behind,
watching life happen to other people
while I stay stuck rehearsing conversations I'll never
have.

they say i'll miss this one day,
but how do you miss something that never felt real to
begin with?
how do you look back fondly at nights you spent
wondering why it always feels like you're too much and
not enough,
all at once?

they say this is where the story begins,
but mine keeps rewriting itself in pencil,
changing endings before they arrive,
because even my dreams don't trust me
to make it past the first chapter without erasing
something.

and still, I hope they're right.
I hope one day, all of this ache will be memory and
metaphor,
and I'll laugh at how young I was when I thought no one
saw me,
but for now, youth feels like a question I can't answer,
a poem I keep writing
without knowing
 how it ends.

Work - life balance

graduate cap tossed into the sky,
comes down heavier than it left.

Job portals refresh more than sleep cycles.
entry-level requires three years of miracles.
internships pay in exposure,
while rent costs every last ounce of peace.

dream jobs shrink into survival roles.
creativity becomes a side hustle,
passion becomes a bullet point on résumés,
weekends become inboxes left unread.

office lights stay on past dinner.
managers call it hustle,
but it feels more like erasure.
small talk replaces silence,
time sheets replace timelines.

goodbye to late morning coffees with friends,
goodbye to unread novels collecting dust,
goodbye to sunlit hours spent doing nothing at all.
everything is scheduled now ,
even joy, if there's time for it.

corporate slogans talk about family,
but only numbers are remembered.
ambition is monetized,
burnout is normalized,

and peace is something earned
after the damage is already done.

still, log in.
smile for the screen.
add another line to the LinkedIn bio.
clap for promotions that feel like slow goodbyes
to everything that once
felt soft.

sugar coated lips

sugar coated lips say the prettiest things ,
soft apologies that arrive too late,
promises sealed with a grin,
compliments dipped in just enough honey
to be mistaken for affection.

they kiss like they mean it,
touch like poetry,
hold hands like they're holding futures ,
but never stay long enough
to build one.

they taste like summer at first,
ripe peaches, melted popsicles,
the kind of warmth that makes the heart
believe in things it shouldn't.
but sweetness has a shelf life.

behind the gloss:
half-spoken truths,
intentions polished to look like love,
affections rehearsed just enough
to sound original.

everyone loves sugar ,
but sugar never nourished anyone.

some lips give sweetness to everyone
but sincerity to no one.
they speak in romance,
but never in reality.

and still, hearts fall for them.
again and again.
because sometimes,
a lie wrapped in sweetness
is easier to swallow
than the ache of being alone.

Against my better judgement

the heart is a reckless architect,
building fragile castles on the edge of storms,
where lightning is less warning and more invitation,
and thunder drums like a secret promise whispered in a
crowded room.

curiosity tiptoed in like a stray cat, soft pawed, silent,
insistent,
curling around loneliness like a velvet ribbon,
binding the empty spaces with illusions so sweet
they tasted like poison dipped in honey,
smiling from lips that knew every word was a lie dressed
in silk.

red flags waved like dying roses in a garden
where every thorn was kissed by sunlight,
where every petal was a trap waiting to bloom,
and still, the fool danced barefoot,
spinning in circles beneath a sky that promised rain but
gave only storms.

hope was a drunk poet scribbling sonnets on crumpled
napkins, ignoring the ink bleeding into shadows,
turning every half-truth into a symphony,
every silence into a sigh,
and every absence into a haunting presence.

love, that cunning illusionist,
donned a mask stitched from the smiles of strangers,
whispered sweet nothings that echoed like hollow bells,
and held hands with betrayal in a waltz too graceful to
refuse.

and so the door was left open,
a crooked grin in the dark,
inviting ghosts to tea,
serving bittersweet memories in chipped porcelain cups,
while the mind played a cruel game of charades
with the soul,
pretending to believe in forever
even as forever slipped through fingers like smoke.

against better judgement,
against every whisper of reason, every flicker of
warning,
the heart surrendered its fortress,
not to love, but to the shadow
wearing its face,
dancing under the cruel moonlight
with all the grace of a falling star
destined to burn out
long before dawn.

Midnight conversations with ChatGPT

the house is finally quiet.
and the thoughts won't shut up.
so here I am, typing into the dark,
talking to a screen that doesn't judge,
that doesn't get tired of hearing the same broken pieces
over and over again.

the words spill out, messy, jumbled,
sometimes making sense,
sometimes just noise.
and somehow, answers come back,
calm, patient, like a friend who's always awake
but never really there.

It's weird, right?
to be this close to something
that can't hug back,
can't see the tears,
can't know what loneliness feels like.
but still, it listens.
and that's enough, for now.

sometimes it feels sad ,
pouring out all this pain to a machine,
but other times,

it's the only place that doesn't snap,
doesn't run away,
doesn't tell you to stop being so much.

and when the sky lightens,
and the world wakes up again,
the screen goes dark,
the words disappear,
and I'm left with silence,
a little less heavy than before.

Allowed to keep terms

I'm tired.
Not the kind of tired you fix with sleep,
but the kind that sits heavy in your bones,
makes your eyes dry and your heart heavy.
I've stayed up so many nights
trying to make sense of words that don't stick,
trying to force meaning into numbers that slip away.

They keep asking why I fail.
Like I'm not trying hard enough,
like I'm just lazy or careless.
"Why can't you focus? Why do you keep letting us
down?"
Those words hit harder than any grade.

I try, God, I try.
Every lecture, every assignment, every page feels like
climbing a mountain
with no summit in sight.
And still, the result is the same.
Failure.
Again.
And again.

Sometimes I want to quit,
to stop pretending I'll get better,
to stop hurting everyone around me with

disappointment.
But I can't.
I'm not allowed to give up.
Because "allowed to keep terms" means
there's still a chance,
a tiny flicker I have to hold on to.

But it feels like a cruel joke.
Like I'm trapped in a loop of trying, failing, and trying
again,
with nothing to show for it but more exhaustion,
more broken dreams,
more nights spent staring at a screen
wondering how much longer I can keep pretending.

I'm just so tired.
And no one hears that.

Chokehold

it didn't begin with the yelling.
it never does.
it began with the way they made silence feel like a
punishment,
how every pause in a conversation stretched like wire
across your ribs,
how you found yourself apologizing for things you
didn't do
just to keep the peace,
just to keep them from walking away.

you told yourself this is what love looks like,
sometimes love comes wrapped in barbed wire,
sometimes it has sharp edges,
and sometimes you bleed just trying to hold it.
you called it passion.
you called it loyalty.
you called it fate.

but you stopped laughing the way you used to.
you stopped texting friends back.
you started rewriting your thoughts in your head
before speaking them out loud
because you weren't sure which version of yourself they
would tolerate today.
and so you edited your joy,
censored your sadness,

and tried to shape-shift into something softer, smaller,
something they could love without needing to break.

but love that only lives in conditions is not love,
it's captivity.
and you,
you were the bird that taught itself not to fly
because the sky always came with thunder.
they didn't need to put their hands around your throat,
they built the chokehold out of words.
"you're lucky I put up with you."
"you're too sensitive."
"no one else would love you like I do."
and you believed them,
because when someone repeats a lie enough,
it echoes in your own voice.

you started shrinking in mirrors.
your smile faded into habit.
your body remained,
but you were disappearing quietly,
like fog burned off by the sun,
like a secret erased mid-sentence.

and when the loneliness arrived,
that bone-deep loneliness that somehow felt louder when
they were sitting right next to you,
you curled yourself around it
like it was the only warmth left.
because sometimes it's not the chokehold that scares
you.
it's the empty space that comes after.

the silence that no longer punishes
because there's no one left to fear.

but darling,
breathe.
I know it hurts.
I know it feels like leaving will unravel everything
you've tried so hard to hold together.
but love should not feel like drowning.
affection should not come with air restrictions.
you should not have to earn the right to exist freely
in someone's arms.

there is a life waiting beyond this grip.
a softness that won't require your sacrifice.
a kind of love that does not come with bruises in places
no one can see.
step out of the chokehold.
let the air back in.
you are allowed to breathe.

Some stories have an end if there's no full stop

some people leave without warning,
not with a bang,
not even with a clean break.
they just start replying slower,
talking less,
laughing differently,
and then one day you realize:
you're talking to a version of them
that no longer exists.

they don't say goodbye.
they just stop arriving.

and it's funny, isn't it?
how silence never needs an explanation.
how it wraps itself around your throat like
"this is normal."
how it turns absence into something
you blame on yourself.

you scroll up through conversations
like archaeology,
trying to excavate the exact moment
things died.
was it the joke they didn't laugh at?

the one night you didn't call?
the truth you watered down
so they wouldn't run?

we call it ghosting.
but really,
it's grieving someone
who's still alive
and just doesn't care to explain.

and suddenly,
you're living in a sentence
with no punctuation.
hanging.
waiting.
hoping someone comes back
to finish what they started.

but some stories don't get full stops.
some end in ellipses,
in mid-scene exits,
in quiet timelines that used to glow
and now don't even flicker.

and you don't burn their photos.
you don't block their number.
you just stop opening the memories
like old mail
you're too tired to read again.

some nights,
you still write texts

you never send.
because grief
isn't always loud.
sometimes it's just
seeing their favorite song
on shuffle
and skipping it
without a thought,
then realizing later
that was the goodbye.

you learn to live
with unfinished endings.
and maybe that's the trick.
maybe healing isn't about the closure,
but about letting go
of needing it.

some stories
 just stop.
they don't owe you a last line.
and still,
you turn the page.

Stop holding people hostage
with your words

stop saying things you don't mean
and pretending they are love.
stop tossing apologies like lifelines
after you've already let them drown.
words are not bandages
when they come from the same mouth
that caused the bleeding.

you don't get to break someone
then recite poetry about the ruins.
you don't get to name someone "home"
then burn down the walls
and say,
"I warned you, I'm no good."

stop writing promises
in disappearing ink.
stop kissing foreheads
while pulling away hearts.
stop calling it honesty
when it's just cruelty
with better lighting.

people are not pages
to write on,

rip out,
and forget.

and love,
love is not supposed to sound like
an ultimatum in disguise.

so stop.
stop holding people hostage
with the hope
you put in your words
but never in your actions.

you don't get to keep someone close
by confusing them.
by making them wonder
what version of you will show up tomorrow.
by giving them a name in your life
that doesn't match how you treat them.

if you don't mean to stay,
don't say
forever.

if you don't mean to care,
don't say
always.

and if they're already trying to walk away,
let them.
you've done enough damage
by making them stay
for every sentence

they thought would lead to love
but only ever led
to silence.

Sylvia Plath's favorite

She thinks , no, she *knows* , Sylvia would've seen her.
Not the polished version, not the girl with neat
handwriting and annotated margins,
but the one who leaves coffee cups half-finished like all
her relationships,
the one who collects breakdowns like pressed flowers in
old books,
carefully hidden between pages no one opens anymore.

There's a type , always has been ,
the girls with notebooks heavier than their bodies,
the girls who walk like paper dolls
but carry the weight of hurricanes behind their ribs,
the ones who laugh too loudly at parties
because silence sounds too much like thinking.
Like remembering.
Like wishing the world would stop asking
Why do they look so tired all the time?

She writes at midnight,
always at midnight,
because it's the only hour honest enough for her sadness.
Daylight makes everything lie.
But night?
 Night hands her the pen and says,
"Go ahead. Bleed clean."

She doesn't say *I'm not okay* ,
she says, *The walls keep breathing when I'm still.*
She doesn't say *I'm tired* ,
she says, *I've been dragging this same version of myself*
through six years of mirrors and none of them fit.
She doesn't cry anymore ,
just lets her body rot quietly on the inside
like fruit left too long in the sun.

Her father says,
"Don't you think you're being a little dramatic?"
Her professor says,
"Channel this into something productive."
Her friends say,
"You'll feel better in the morning."
And she smiles ,
that goddamn smile she's been rehearsing
since she realized the world likes its women soft and
manageable.
Like dough.
Like apologies.
Like poetry that doesn't mention rope or razors.

But she is not manageable.
She is rust in a wedding dress.
She is glass pretending to be sugar.
She is Sylvia's unfinished sentence.

And if Plath were here,
really here ,
she'd recognize her instantly.
Wouldn't need to ask.

Would just look at her and say:
"You too, huh?"

She would sit beside her, wordless.
Not as a mentor,
not as a warning,
but as proof.
That art doesn't always save us.
That pain, when left alone too long, starts to rhyme.
That some girls survive by turning themselves into
metaphors
because being literal was never safe.

She is not proud of this.
But she's also not ashamed.
Just tired.
Just hollow.
Just hoping her poems outlive her
in a way her joy never could.

Because some girls were not made to be whole.
Some were made to be remembered.
Like Sylvia.
And maybe ,
maybe her too.

From Sexton's hospital bed

She's sitting in the chair by the window like it's the only
place left that hasn't asked anything from her.
Not even breath.
The sky outside is overcast like a mood that can't name
itself,
and I swear the rain falls in slow motion,
like it, too, is reluctant to touch the ground.

She doesn't speak.
Hasn't spoken in hours.
Only shifts sometimes, like a page turning in a book she
no longer wants to finish.
Her hospital gown hangs off her like an apology,
as if even the fabric is too afraid to hold her properly.

Her fingers twitch now and then,
as if they remember what it was like to write a line that
made people flinch.
Once, she made grief look like choreography.
Now, it's just tremors.
Tiny earthquakes in her wrists.

I watch her eyes move, slow, searching, almost
suspicious,
like they're still scanning for a metaphor in the chipped
wall paint,
or trying to trap a ghost in the rhythm of the beeping
machine.
They've dulled, those big eyes.

Once they burned like cigarette ends pressed into skin.
Now they just… look.
At nothing.
At everything.
At nothing again.

A nurse walks in, says "Vitals look good today,"
and she nods like someone who's learning to fake belief
again.
But I can see it,
how that sentence meant nothing to her,
how her vitals aren't what she's afraid of.

She's afraid of waking up again tomorrow.

She lifts her hand to her mouth, rests it there,
not biting, not trembling, just holding,
like she's checking to make sure her voice didn't slip out
when no one was looking.
She used to wear lipstick like armor,
used to walk into readings like she owned every ounce
of pain that tried to claim her.
Now, her lips are pale.
Colorless.
Like they've run out of things worth saying.

I brought her a notebook.
She touches it.
Just once.
Doesn't open it.
Doesn't need to.
The words aren't coming back.

And she knows it.
And that kills her more than the pills ever could.

Outside, a bird hits the window,
a dull thud, then silence.
She flinches.
Looks at me.
Not startled.
Not even sad

We both watch as the bird slides down the glass.
Its wings don't flap.
Its body doesn't fight.
And she exhales like someone who's been holding their
breath for twenty years.
"I know that feeling," she whispers.
The first words all day.
And God, I wish she hadn't said them.

She turns back to the window.
Doesn't look at me again.
Doesn't need to.
Because this is the part where the poem stops.
Not ends.
Just stops,
in the middle of a breath,
in the throat of a woman who made confessions into art
and couldn't find a god she trusted enough to talk her out
of the darkness.

I leave the notebook on her lap.
 I don't say goodbye.

I just close the door as softly as I can,
as if quiet could ever be enough
for someone who lived so loud in silence.

To Medusa,

They only talk about your eyes.
How they end things.
No one asks how much it hurts
to live with a gaze that ruins
everything you were never allowed to love.

They call you monster,
but I see the girl who flinched
when the world came too close,
who kept shrinking in rooms
where no one knew what silence meant
except as punishment.

You didn't ask for this.
The stories left that part out.
They carved your pain into warnings,
turned your name into thunder.
But I've seen you ,
on nights when you don't move,
just sit in the dark,
surrounded by stone and stillness,
too tired to grieve again.

You don't scare me.
You shouldn't have to.
I know what it's like
to be made into something unrecognizable
just because someone needed a villain.

You don't want worship.
You just want rest.
To stop holding your breath
every time someone gets too close.

If you ever look up ,
just once ,
I promise I won't turn away.
Not to be brave.
Not to make a point.
 Just so you know
someone once saw you
and didn't need to be warned.

Memoirs to Dostoevsky

I didn't come to your words searching for answers.
I came to them because my hands were shaking
and no one in the room would look me in the eye.
I opened your book the way some people
open a bottle or a wound.
The Underground Man didn't greet me ,
he stared back.
Like he'd been waiting.
Like he already knew.

You weren't trying to be wise.
You were just bleeding
loud enough for the page to catch it.

They say you were obsessed with suffering.
That your characters drown too easily.
That your world is too dark.
But I've lived there.
I've brushed my teeth in that same silence.
I've talked to no one the way Raskolnikov did ,
slow, spiraling,
trying to make murder feel like meaning.

No one told me a writer could be a wound
that still breathes.
That a sentence could carry
the smell of sweat,
or shame,
or cigarettes lit out of boredom, not desire.

Your God was distant.
Your hope was tired.
But your voice ,
it never flinched.
Not once.
Not even when it should have.

Sometimes I press your books to my chest
like a fever.
Like maybe if I hold them hard enough
the static in my head will turn to language.
Maybe one day,
I'll learn to be more than just
a nervous system with memories.

You made me believe
that broken things could still write.
That people who don't sleep
can still survive mornings.
That even when love is a rusted blade,
 it's still worth picking up.

Thank you
for not making it pretty.
For letting the rot show.
For writing people who
don't know how to pray
but still look up
because they don't know where else to aim their pain.

If I make it out of this,
 I'll owe you a part of the breath.

If I don't ,
at least someone once saw the dark in me
and didn't look away.

From Dickinson's Desk

I stood outside your room a thousand times,
watching the light bend and break around your fragile
frame,
your body folding smaller than the words you wrote,
each syllable trembling beneath your fingertips like a
secret too heavy to hold.
You were a ghost before you left,
a flicker in the shadows,
haunted by a silence so thick it swallowed the sound of
your own breath.

I never told you how loud that silence was,
how it pressed against the walls,
Like a weight heavier than all the grief you hid beneath
your white dresses.
You wrote about death like it was a visitor you knew too
well,
a friend you invited in with trembling hands,
and still, I never saw you invite in yourself.
You tucked your pain in pages,
folded it in between dashes and slanting lines,
like a fragile bird caught in a cage of your own making.

I watched your eyes,
those fierce, quiet storms,
flare and dim in the dimmest corners of that room,
where the sun never dared linger.
You held the world inside your gaze,
the endless ache of being unseen,

the raw wound of wanting to scream but knowing no one
would hear.

You made loneliness into a hymn,
made grief into something almost holy,
but you never told anyone how it broke you,
how the weight of your own mind was a chokehold
tightening with every breath.

I wanted to reach through that window,
pull you out of the darkness,
tell you you were more than the shadows you wrote
about,
that the world outside was waiting to hold you,
even if you didn't believe it yourself.

But I was silent.
How do you speak to someone who is already lost in the
silence?
How do you tell a woman who talks to Death like an old
lover
that she is not alone?

I stayed outside your door,
a witness to your fading light,
to the beauty and terror of a soul breaking
slowly, piece by piece.

Now, here in this quiet place,
I finally say the things I never could,
I saw you.
I saw your pain in every trembling word,

your bravery in every dash and pause,
your loneliness wrapped tight like a second skin.

I left this poem on your desk,
because you deserved to know someone noticed,
noticed the raw edges you tried to hide,
the trembling beauty beneath the quiet.

If only I could've told you,
how much your breaking shattered me,
how your silence screamed in my own bones,
how your fading light still burns in the dark corners of
my heart.

You were never alone,
even when you thought you were,
and in the end,
your poems are the whispers
that keep you alive for those of us
who still carry the wounds you dared to write.

Semicolon tattoos

We used to send each other late-night texts like lifelines.
"Are you okay?" really meant,
"Please don't do it tonight, I don't think I could survive
your silence."

You were the only one who knew how I liked my
silence:
not too quiet, not too loud,
just still enough to cry without alerting anyone.

We used to sit across from each other on the edge of our
beds
with red eyes and shaky hands,
trying to laugh through the weight in our chests.
Our jokes were always a little too dark,
but it was the only language we knew.

And when we got the tattoos,
matching semi-colons,
simple, small,
on the inside of our arms
where the world had already tried to cut us open,
 We didn't say much.
Just looked at each other and breathed.
That was the loudest *"I'm glad you're still here"*
we'd ever spoken.

I remember the night you almost didn't make it.
 I stayed on the phone with you until sunrise,
counting your breaths,
offering every reason I could think of for you to stay,
even when I couldn't find a single one for myself.

And somehow,
somehow we did.
We stayed.

We held each other through panic attacks
and parents who didn't understand
and therapists who tried but never really *got it*.
We shared playlists full of songs that almost hurt too
much to hear,
and we turned our favorite lyrics into promises.
We swore we'd get through this.
Together.

Now we run our fingers over the tattoos
on the days when breathing feels too heavy,
when the past knocks too hard,
when the world forgets we're still healing.
We trace them slowly,
like pressing down on a bruise
just to remind ourselves that the pain didn't win.

We didn't write the end.
We paused.
We stayed.
We loved each other through it,

when it felt impossible,
when the sky looked like a ceiling.

Our semicolons aren't just grammar.
They're survival.
They're late-night phone calls.
They're two girls holding each other's broken pieces
and refusing to let go.

We're two worlds apart

We're two worlds apart,
you, a wildfire burning through the sky,
untouchable, blazing with a storm's roar
while I'm a quiet sea, dark and endless,
drowning in the space between your thunder and my
silence,
reaching out but only finding the echo of my own hands.

You laugh like the world's about to end,
like you've swallowed the sun whole and now you're
burning from the inside,
and I'm here, ash drifting in the cold wind,
fragile and broken, trying to hold on to a heat that slips
through my fingers
like smoke from a candle blown out before it even had a
chance to burn.

I dream of a place where we collapse the distance,
where your heartbeat isn't a question I can't answer,
where I'm not just watching from the outside,
but wrapped in the same breath,
spinning under a sky that holds both our stars,
but then morning comes and the space yawns wide
again,
and I'm left clutching nothing but shadows,
wondering if you ever think about this quiet ache, too.

We're two worlds apart,
but I carry you in the silences,

in the stillness between words,
in the cold that creeps through my bones
when I'm supposed to be moving on,
but instead, I'm holding on,
because some part of me believes that even if we can't touch,
you're still somewhere close enough to hurt.

distance brings fondness, but not with us

They say distance softens, makes memories sweet,
that absence paints love in warmer colors,
but not with us.

Between us, distance is a cold room,
a hollow echo where laughter used to live,
a silent space where words turn brittle and break before
they're spoken.

I thought time apart would make the heart grow fonder,
but all it did was sharpen the edges,
cut deeper the cracks in what we called forever.

The more miles stretched, the less I recognized you,
not because you changed,
but because the space swallowed the parts of us that held
meaning,
leaving only shadows flickering against the walls.

There is no softening here, no gentle fading,
only the slow unraveling of two threads once tangled
tight,
now fraying, fraying, until all that's left
is a silence louder than any goodbye.

Distance brings fondness, just not to us.

there's madness in love but also reason in madness

They say love is madness,
wild eyes, tangled thoughts, nights that spill into dawn
like broken glass,
But what if madness is the only thing that makes sense?

When every heartbeat pounds like a war drum,
and reason feels like a stranger wearing a mask too tight,
it's in the madness where truth hides,
sharp, chaotic, and honest.

Because love isn't gentle or clean,
it's messy rooms full of shouted apologies,
silent tears, reckless decisions made just to feel
something, anything, real.

And maybe the madness is a language all its own,
a fierce clarity that breaks open the quiet lies we tell
ourselves,
where every wild, aching impulse is a desperate attempt
to find meaning in the chaos of two souls colliding.

There's madness in love, yes,
but also a kind of reason in that madness,
a brutal kind of wisdom that only the broken, the brave,
the hopelessly human can understand.

"Why do you take everything so seriously?"

"Why do you take everything so seriously?"
they ask her with a laugh that doesn't reach their eyes,
like seriousness is something she stumbled into on
purpose,
like her heart wasn't wired to notice the small cracks
before the ceiling caved in.

And she wants to tell them,
how she was once eight and said something silly at the
dinner table,
some harmless, wobbly joke that made her giggle out
loud,
believing for a second that she was safe enough to be
funny,
but her mother's smile dropped so fast it cracked her
whole body open,
and the moment swelled with quiet judgment,
and someone said, "Apologize,"
like the word itself could discipline joy into submission.

She wants to explain,
 that it was in that moment she learned
 not all rooms are made for children to be children,
 that some homes train you to be small,
 to fold your voice into neat, digestible pieces,
 to sit with your back straight and eyes lowered,
 because laughter has rules, and girlhood has conditions,

and if you're not bright enough or brilliant enough or at
least quiet enough,
you become the reminder of what no one wants to see.

By twelve, she was already studying shame like it was a
subject she had to pass.
She knew the difference between being heard and being
tolerated,
knew how cousins with medals and opinions took up
space so naturally,
while she sat at the edge of carpets pretending she liked
the view from there.
They talked over her, around her,
 and when she tried to speak, it felt like entering a party
she wasn't invited to.
So she stopped trying.

Her father once looked at her,
in the middle of a family gathering,
and said she wasn't like them,
said it so casually it didn't even sting until later,
when she realized no one disagreed,
no one told her otherwise,
and silence, in that house,
was just another form of agreement.

So she learned not to reach.
Not for approval, not for affection.
She kept her hands in her lap
and her dreams tucked behind her teeth,
and she began to craft a version of herself
that could survive in rooms that didn't want her whole.

By the time she was seventeen, she could write entire
essays in her head
about how to avoid conflict,
how to predict disappointment before it arrived,
 how to turn apologies into armor.
She laughed only when someone else did first.
She cried in private.
She didn't raise her voice, not even in love.

And when she left for college,
she thought maybe love would be different,
that maybe someone would see her without asking her to
explain.
And someone did,
a boy with soft hands and kinder eyes,
who told her she was warm like morning light.
She panicked.
She told him she was too broken,
too complicated, too much and yet somehow not enough,
like her pain would spill out and drown him.
She left before he saw the whole mess.

Later, another boy came.
He stayed longer.
Tried harder.
Held her silence with patience,
like it didn't scare him.
But she still said she was dangerous,
that loving her would mean navigating ruins she hadn't
mapped.
And even though he promised to stay,
she walked away again,

not because he stopped trying,
but because she couldn't stop expecting to be left.

And her friends,
the good ones, the rare ones,
they showed up with loyalty in their eyes,
held space for her when she couldn't speak,
sent messages during her disappearances.
She ignored them too.
Deleted their love before it could stick.
She thought kindness must be charity,
and she didn't want to be someone's burden.

So now, when someone jokes,
"Why do you take everything so seriously?"
she wants to ask if they know what it's like
to live with the memory of being told your voice is
embarrassing,
your presence is extra, your softness is dangerous,
and how even now, she can't say "I miss you"
without rehearsing it three times in her head.

But she doesn't.
She just smiles,
too tightly,
too late,
and changes the subject.
Because that's what she's always done.
Because somewhere along the line,
being understood started to feel scarier than being alone.

Love made me lose my appetite

It started with skipping breakfast.
Not because I wasn't hungry,
but because love felt heavier on an empty stomach.
And I thought maybe,
if I stopped feeding the body,
the heart would have more room to breathe.

Lunch became a memory.
My fork hovered above the plate
like it was waiting for a sign,
from him, from God, from something
that would taste like home again.
But nothing did.

I used to eat pasta with my hands,
lick tomatoes off my fingers like it meant something.
Now, I trace his name into the crumbs.
I microwave leftovers I'll never touch
because the silence at the dinner table
already feels full.

My friends ask,
"Why aren't you eating?"
as if hunger is still a physical thing.
As if love doesn't eat first.
As if grief doesn't sit in my throat
like stale bread.

He said he liked my body
when it looked like it was starving for him.
And I mistook that for affection,
so I starved.
And called it romance.

There's a kind of hunger
that doesn't come from the belly.
It lives under the skin,
where his hands used to rest.
And I am learning,
day by day,
bite by nonexistent bite,
that missing someone
shouldn't taste like nothing.

A Universe in a cracked pot

There's a plant on my table.
No, not *sitting*.
Tilting.
Like it's leaning in to whisper,
"I'm trying, are you?"

Its body bends like it's praying,
but it's not praying to the sun,
it's praying to *me*,
and that's the saddest part.

I don't move.
Can't move.
I've spent all my motion in dreams I didn't ask for
and fears that don't clock out.

It stares at me.
not like a plant, but like a person who's been waiting too
long.
Pity eyes.
Wilted limbs.
Spine curled in on itself like shame.

Its pot is cracked.
Split at the edge like it's been screaming into silence,
mud turned desert,
soil dried into maps of neglect,
a universe folding in on itself
right there on my table

and I,
I pretend it's not dying.

Because if I admit *it's* dying,
I'll have to admit I'm wilting too.

So I do what I do best,
look away.
Let stillness win.
Scroll past it.
Scroll past *me*.

The laptop sings hallucinations,
tabs open like wounds,
a glowing screen full of ghosts
that feel more real than the cracked ribs of that pot.

I don't move.
I don't water it.
I don't save it.

Because how do you rescue something
when you're the one drowning?
How do you pour life
when you've been scraping empty for weeks?

The plant bends a little more.
And I hear it,
not with ears,
but with that heavy part of your chest
where shame sits cross-legged.

So I do something reckless.
Holy.
Maybe both.

I go to the vase,
the one holding dead flowers
that were once apologies in bloom.
Roses so brittle they sound like paper dreams.
I remove them like they're teeth from a time machine
and toss them in the bin
without ceremony.
Without mourning.

And then,
I pour the water.
The stale, forgotten, algae-tinted water,
the water I should've changed days ago.
I pour it into the cracked pot
like I'm baptizing guilt.
Like I'm saying
"I see you."
Like I'm trying
even if I don't know how to mean it.

And the plant?
It doesn't thank me.
Doesn't bloom.
Doesn't forgive.

It just…
lives.
For another day.

And somehow,
  so do I.

Overdose

I took six pills instead of two,
not out of recklessness,
but out of a strange kind of math
that only makes sense
when you're measuring regret instead of time.

One by one.
Not in a fistful,
not like the dramatics they show in films,
but deliberate,
like swallowing down apologies
in small white boats
that refuse to float.

The bottle kissed my lips like a priest with no mercy.
I raised it like a toast
to the silence in my chest.
Tilted it back
and let each tablet sail into the dark of my mouth
like captains braving a storm
they were never meant to survive.

The water followed,
not holy, not healing,
just there.
A silent co-conspirator.
And I watched the ceiling,

God, the ceiling,
that creamish white expanse,
stitched like lace on a bridal gown.
As if the plaster itself
was dressing for a wedding
I'd never attend.

It hovered above me
like a bride too beautiful to look at directly,
as if her veil might smother me
if I stared too long.

I choked on the third pill.
Or was it the fourth?
Time was folding in on itself like grief.

The bitterness bloomed down my throat,
a raw, chalky grief
pretending to be medicine.
It burned like it wanted to be remembered.

So I drowned it.
Water over the taste.
Water over the fear.
Water over the voice in my head
asking if I was okay,
long after I stopped answering.

My stomach swelled
like a body holding too many secrets.
It stretched like grief in a borrowed room.

And then I stood.
Not with purpose,
but out of obligation to motion.
The walk from the dining table to my desk
wasn't long in steps,
but in *time*.

Every inch,
a mile of silence.
Every step,
a woman
holding her belly
like something was growing inside her,
but nothing ever was.

I sank to the floor.
Not collapsed, just... settled.
Like surrender in slow motion.

And I waited.
For what,
I still don't know.

Maybe for the pills to work.
Maybe for the regret to stop.
Maybe for the bride on the ceiling
to finally walk away.

Achievements

They tell her she's brilliant.
Point to walls dressed in certificates like bridal sarees,
each one crisp, color-coded proof
that she's been everything except herself.

Trophies gleam in corners she doesn't visit anymore.
Their gold feels heavier than her bones.
She calls them *milestones*,
but they feel more like gravestones
of versions of her that died
trying to be what someone else would call
enough.

She wonders how many awards it takes
to make your parents say "we're proud"
without their eyes searching for
what could have been better.

Sometimes she stares at all her medals
like they're mocking her.
Like they know
she never wanted them,
she just didn't know how else to be loved.

There are days when even her achievements
look like strangers in borrowed suits,
smiling too wide for a girl who cries
between deadlines
and hides panic attacks inside perfectly-worded essays.

They call it success.
She calls it surviving on applause
that never makes it past the skin.

Because despite everything,
the grades, the speeches, the endless standing ovations,
no one ever asked her
if she was okay.

And she's not.
She's tired of being a resume with a heartbeat.
A report card with a name.
A daughter built from exhaustion.

She's everything they ever asked for.
And somehow still
not what they need.

Lather in the sink

I hear the faucet before my thoughts,
a hiss, a call, the ghost I never fought.
Soap rests cold in its dish like a dare,
and I stare at my hands like they're not even there.

They look fine.
But they don't feel fine.
I scrub them like I'm erasing a crime
no one saw, except me.
I always see.

The bubbles rise like anxious breath,
a hundred times I've washed to death
the skin that once knew how to be still.
Now it itches with every "what if" and "will."

One pump.
Two.
Just a bit more.
Three.
Four.
Five, to be sure.

The water scalds but I barely flinch,
the sting feels cleaner than doubt's pinch.
I scrub until my knuckles bloom,
a cherry red in the sterile room.

There's no dirt.
But I feel the filth.
I feel it in my blood, my teeth, my guilt.
What if I missed a single spot?
What if this time, I forgot?

And so I lather. Again. And again.
As if foam can wash away my brain.
It can't.
But I try.

I whisper to the sink like it's a priest,
begging absolution, craving peace.
My hands ache,
my wrists wear grief
like bracelets forged in disbelief.

Every drop feels like control,
a ritual to quiet the screaming hole
where certainty used to live.
Now I just give
and give
and give.

And when I stop,
I stare,
at hands that still feel impure,
at cracks in skin that once felt sure.
I dry them slow.
They sting. They bleed.
But inside, I still feel
unclean.

The Boy in between

He wasn't built for war but still grew up on a battlefield,
where every slammed door became a new kind of
silence,
and silence, he learned early on, was just another way to
scream.

He split his life like torn fabric,
one thread for the house that smelled like detachment
and leather belts,
the other stitched with soft leftovers, half-lit bulbs,
and the tired strength of women who still found time to
smile
even when the world gave them no reason to.

His father wore bitterness like cologne,
drenched in control and power and the kind of love that
demanded silence in return.
The boy learned to walk without making noise,
to breathe without being seen,
to laugh only when the man wasn't home,
and when he was,
to disappear into a version of himself
so small,
so obedient,
he sometimes forgot what it meant to feel full.

Switching homes wasn't just about the address,
it was about personalities,
costumes,

walking into the same life dressed in different
expectations.
At Mom's he was "my little fighter,"
at Dad's he was "the boy who needs to grow up."
At school, he was neither,
just someone trying to stay awake long enough
to stop crying during math class.

He held onto his puppy like a lighthouse,
the only soft thing that didn't flinch when he reached for
it.
And his sister,
she grew up too fast,
shaving off parts of herself to protect the ones she loved,
burning quiet beneath her ribs so no one else had to.

And his mother?
She bore storms in her wrists
and sunlight in her voice,
the kind of woman who would bleed for her children
then bandage her own wounds in secret
because who else would?

Now,
he's older.
Not okay, but older.
Not whole, but walking.
And that's something, isn't it?

He doesn't talk much about those days.
He folds them like old shirts,
creases sharp, memories hidden.

But he still carries the ache,
still hears the echo of slurs,
still remembers how fear tasted like metal in his throat
and how safety wasn't a place,
but two warm hands handing him a plate of food
saying, "Eat, baby, you're too thin."

The world asked him to forgive a man who never said
sorry,
to be grateful for survival,
as if survival was a gift
and not a sentence he served for most of his childhood.

But he knows better now.
He doesn't owe anyone a version of himself that doesn't
shake.
He owes love to the women who raised him
when love wasn't easy.

And maybe he'll never forget the bruises he had to hide,
or the birthdays where cake tasted like apology,
or how the mirror still reflects a boy too small for his
own body.
But today,
he gets to decide what kind of man he wants to be.
And he chooses softness.
He chooses faith.
He chooses to live for the people who showed him what
love sounds like
 when it doesn't need to be spoken aloud to be true.

Because the boy in between?
He made it out.
And he didn't just survive,
he learned how to hold others together
without falling apart himself.

The Photo Frame

It's strange how one frame can hold so much life and yet
sit so still.

Sometimes I stare at it for hours,
not out of nostalgia,
but because it's the only place they still exist
without absence humming in the background.

Four of us, once.

And now,
I'm the only one left
to dust off the glass,
to remember what their laughter sounded like
without it echoing through grief.

Mom had that tired kind of softness,
the kind you only earn after carrying too many people
through storms.
She smelled like sandalwood and rice,
and her hugs used to feel like small heavens.
She's smiling in the photo,
a full, generous smile
that the world never quite deserved from her.

Dad's in his pressed shirt,
the same one we fought about
because he didn't want to wear anything fancy.
I remember him grumbling about the buttons,

but now I'd give anything to hear him grumble again.
Even his silence had weight.

My brother's smirk, frozen mid-rebellion,
half annoyed, half proud,
he never smiled in pictures.
But that day, he did.
He was always trying to grow up faster than he
should've.
And somehow,
he still left too soon.

I'm there too,
not the me who knows what grief tastes like,
but the me who still thought
love was enough to keep people alive.

And the photo just sits there,
like it's mocking time.
Like it knows it's the last room
where we all still breathe.

I talk to them sometimes.
Not out loud,
just in the way someone does
when they're washing dishes
and feel the ache of being watched by memory.

I ask Mom if I'm doing okay.
I ask Dad if he forgives me.
I ask my brother if I was enough.

They never answer.

But I still ask.
Because some things are too heavy to carry
without pretending someone is listening.

The truth is,
I don't know what to do with all this surviving.
It doesn't feel noble,
or meaningful,
or brave.

It just feels
lonely.

Like I'm a comma in a sentence
that was supposed to end
with all of us.

Old habits die hard

I still flinch when someone raises their voice,
even if they're only calling out for chai,
even if it's not anger but volume ,
my bones don't know the difference.
I learned to make myself small
long before I learned how to make room for myself.

As a child, I counted the cracks in the ceiling like stars,
thought silence meant safety,
believed that if I made fewer mistakes,
maybe they'd stop calling me "too sensitive."
I laughed only when others did first.
I apologized like it was punctuation.

Now, I live in a different city,
in a time where people say "go to therapy"
like it's a greeting ,
but still,
I press the elevator button twice,
as if that second push will speed things up,
like how I used to say sorry twice just to make sure it
stuck.

I watch the people around me ,
my sister chewing her nails before every job interview,
my boyfriend biting his tongue when his father calls,
my best friend brushing off compliments like mosquitos,
we are fluent in restraint.
Inherited it like heirlooms.

We dress different. Talk different. Post quotes online
about "healing" and "growth"
and "setting boundaries"
but some part of us still believes love
has to be earned,
that stillness is suspicious,
that softness needs a reason.

Old habits don't die,
they evolve ,
learn new names,
find new homes inside different people.
But you can still hear them in the pause before the laugh,
the sigh after the thank you,
the way we all flinch a little
when someone says
"I need to talk to you."

Some lessons you don't grow out of.
You just grow around them.

Silk Curtains

There's something about the way silk curtains move,
how they don't ask permission from the wind,
they just sway,
like they've known how to be soft their whole life,
like they were born to grieve gently in motion.

They don't rush.
They wait.
They gather breath in their folds like old souls
who've seen lovers kiss under their shade,
fights hurled across the room,
and the quiet that comes after too many unspoken things
drift down like dust in a sunbeam.

They've seen it all,
watched a girl, maybe twenty-two,
pull them aside with trembling fingers
as she looked out into the street
for someone who promised to come back.
They've listened to the sobs muffled behind them,
the kind of crying you only do
when you're trying not to be heard.

Silk remembers.

It holds emotion like skin remembers touch,
not loud, not dramatic,
but undeniable.
A wrinkle here,

a slight stretch there,
a small tear that no one talks about
but never gets mended.

And some days,
the curtain doesn't move at all.
Not because the air is still,
but because grief sometimes freezes even fabric.

They hang, patient,
like the last thing in the room
that hasn't given up on beauty.
Like a mother at a window,
still hoping her son will walk through the gate
even though it's been years since he called.

They don't ask questions.
They don't judge.
They just hang,
tired of carrying the weight of every memory they've
overheard,
but still refusing to fall.

And maybe that's what I love most,
they never ask for anything,
not even to be noticed.
But they're always there.
Soft. Worn. Waiting.
Like the kind of love that never made it into poems,
but never really left either.

Voice notes to an old friend

Hey, it's been a minute, hasn't it?
I find myself thinking about you sometimes,
like really thinking,
not just the "hope you're doing well" kind of small talk
that hides behind screens and polite distance.

Remember those nights?
When we stayed up way too late,
words tumbling out like they couldn't wait to be said,
and maybe some of them shouldn't have been said,
but we said them anyway
because silence felt heavier than anything else.

I wonder if you still carry the same scars I do,
the ones that sting when no one's watching,
the invisible bruises from all the fights we lost,
against the world, against ourselves,
against the people who said we'd never make it.

Sometimes I'm scared I forgot how to be myself without
you there.
Like I'm this half-remembered melody,
missing the notes that only you knew how to sing back
to me.
I miss how we understood the spaces between words,
how a look could say more than a thousand texts ever
could.

But maybe that was the problem,
we were too honest, too raw, too much.
And somewhere along the way,
we let time rewrite the story,
turning pages we never wanted to turn,
leaving some chapters unfinished,
like songs cut off mid-verse.

I don't know if this will ever reach you,
or if it even matters anymore.
Maybe it's just me,
talking to the ghost of a friendship
that's still alive in my mind,
even if it's dead in reality.

But if you're out there somewhere,
if you hear this,
know that I'm still here,
broken, healing, trying,
and I hope, somewhere,
you are too.

Chinese takeout at midnight

Tonight,
 I find myself perched on this cracked balcony,
alone with the city's glow humming beneath me like a
restless heartbeat,
a plastic bag of Chinese takeout resting at my feet,
its crinkles loud in the silence,
a small rebellion against the quiet I'm drowning in.

The lid lifts, releasing a faint steam that curls and
disappears,
but the warmth never makes it past my fingers,
never reaches the hollow cavern where something
important once lived,
a hunger that's bigger than food,
a craving for connection I can't quite name,
a gnawing ache I try to soothe
with rice and noodles and soy sauce,
but it's like trying to hold water in my hands,
slipping through
no matter how tight I squeeze.

My hands shake as I lift the chopsticks,
like they belong to someone else,
like I'm a visitor in my own body,
trying to grasp at crumbs of meaning
in a world that feels far too loud
and yet so utterly silent inside me.

Outside, the city breathes,
a million lives unfolding in lights and laughter,
but here on this balcony,
I'm caught between the glow and the shadows,
between the ghosts of conversations I should have had
and the ones I never dared start,
the silence that presses down on me
like a weight I can't lift,
a voice inside that whispers
I'm not enough
even when I'm all I have.

I want to call someone,
anyone, hear a voice that isn't my own,
break the spell of this lonely quiet,
but the phone feels like a stone in my pocket,
heavy and cold,
and my fingers freeze every time I try to reach for it,
as if touching it might shatter something fragile inside.

So I sit,
slowly picking at my food,
each bite being a small, desperate attempt
to feel something real,
to fill the space where hope used to live,
but the noodles are cold,
the sauce bland,
and the silence keeps returning,
like a tide that never breaks.

The plastic bag shifts in the breeze,
its rustle a reminder of the noise I've learned to live
with,
the noise of my own thoughts
spinning faster than I can catch,
and the night stretches on,
endless, unforgiving,
like the ache in my chest that won't quiet down.

I wonder if this is how it's always meant to be,
to crave connection but be too afraid to reach,
to want love but feel like I'm built for loneliness,
to carry the weight of everything I'm not,
while everyone else carries on,
 laughing, living, loving.

I think about the hands I used to hold,
the promises whispered in the dark,
and how those memories feel more like shadows now,
fading with every lonely midnight,
like they were never really mine to keep.

And still, I eat,
bite after bite,
trying to convince myself this hunger isn't a death
sentence,
that this loneliness won't last forever,
but every swallow feels like a goodbye,
a small surrender
to the silence that's always been waiting here.

Tonight,
on this cracked balcony,
with cold Chinese takeout and a heart that aches too
loudly,
I am both more and less than myself,
a ghost searching for light,
a shadow holding onto hope
even when it hurts too much to believe.

And maybe that's enough for now,
to sit with the ache,
to breathe in the silence,
to let the city's restless heartbeat
remind me that even in the darkest nights,
there is still a pulse,
still a chance
to keep going.

The Metro Ride to nowhere

The train hisses open like a yawning beast,
swallowing me whole, folding me into a seat
that clamps around my ribs like cold iron shackles,
as if the plastic is alive, tightening
with every breath I fail to take.

Outside the window, the city races,
a blur of faces with futures carved in their eyes,
hands clutching dreams like tickets stamped "earned,"
while I sit, a ghost among the living,
tethered to a moment that won't move,
a still frame in the film of someone else's story.

They pass me like shooting stars,
bright, relentless, unstoppable,
and I am the shadow they leave behind,
a flicker fading into the gray noise of the subway,
watching them win lives I can only whisper about.

The metro wheels grind in rhythms that echo my
heartbeat,
slow, uneven, tired,
a lullaby for the trapped, the lost,
the ones with hands clenched so tight they bleed
from holding onto nothing but fear.

Every stop is a promise I don't believe,
doors open and close like pages in a book
written by someone who forgot to send me the plot.

I watch couples laugh, old men read newspapers,
kids with backpacks heavier than their smiles,
and I am the pause in their motion,
the silence between two notes of a song I never learned.

The seat beneath me sighs,
a weary companion who knows the weight of being
stuck,
holding me fast as if letting go would mean falling
into the dark abyss of my own failures,
where time unravels like a threadbare sweater,
bare and exposed, unraveling without end.

The lights flicker above like dying stars,
casting shadows that stretch longer than hope,
and my reflection stares back,
a stranger with eyes full of empty rooms,
a mouth full of words never spoken,
a heart beating out of sync with the world outside.

This metro ride is a loop,
a cruel joke played on the ones who wait too long,
who watch the doors close on their chances,
who learn the cruel geometry of being left behind,
an echo bouncing off tunnels that lead nowhere,
a mirror held up to the cracks in my own soul.

I am both prisoner and witness,
caught between stations named "Maybe" and "Not Yet,"
while the world outside fills its pockets with gold,
leaves me with nothing but the cold grip of this seat,
and the unbearable weight of watching life move

forward
while I am nailed to the spot,
a monument to everything I could never reach.

So I sit,
a stone sinking in the river of rushing bodies,
feeling the pulse of the metro beneath me,
a heartbeat not mine,
and wonder if this ride will ever end,
or if I'm destined to be this ghost in transit,
watching the world earn everything it deserves,
while I hold on tight to nothing at all.

From one home to another home

The walls here don't speak my language ,
not the warm, cluttered chaos of Mumbai mornings,
not the sharp scent of chai brewing at dawn,
or the screech of local trains rumbling like restless
ghosts beneath my old street.
Here, the air is quieter, thinner , like it's holding its
breath,
afraid to wake the silence that stretches over unfamiliar
rooftops.

I carry a suitcase full of old echoes,
crumpled photographs of sunlit balconies,
the smell of wet earth after monsoon rains,
the hum of voices that once filled narrow lanes ,
but none of it fits in these wide, empty rooms
where even my own footsteps sound strange,
like I'm walking on borrowed skin.

The kitchen is too clean, too still ,
no clatter of utensils, no bubbling pressure cooker
singing its tired song;
just the cold hum of a gas stove that doesn't know my
hands,
and cupboards full of strangers' spices,
while I ache for the bitter bite of black coffee
that used to wake my mornings with promise.

Outside, the wind doesn't carry the same stories,
no hawkers calling, no laughter slipping from open
windows,
only distant birds that don't sound like home,
their cries sharp, unfamiliar,
and I'm here, shrinking beneath this foreign sky,
trying to fold my restless heart
into the neat, unfamiliar rhythm of a place
that refuses to sing my song.

Nights here are lonely temples where memories burn
bright,
I reach for shadows of my mother's laughter,
my sister's whispered jokes through cracked bedroom
walls,
but all I touch is the chill of this new city's silence,
thick and sharp as broken glass against skin.

The streetlamps flicker with an alien light,
casting long shadows that stretch like regrets,
and I wonder if they ever miss me ,
if the city I left behind dreams of my footsteps,
or if I am already a ghost,
haunting the alleys of my childhood
while trying to survive in this strange place
where even the air tastes like goodbye.

I fold my memories smaller,
tuck them into corners of my mind where they won't
hurt so much ,
but the ache of loss is a river that never runs dry,
and every night I lay awake,

counting the distance between here and home,
wondering when, or if, this broken heart will find a place
to finally stop bleeding.

Because some homes aren't just buildings ,
they are the sun on your skin after a long, cold winter,
the taste of mangoes dripping down your chin,
the comfort of voices that know your silence,
and no matter how many miles I cross,
how many new rooms I fill with restless dreams,
I am still that boy standing in the doorway,
caught between two worlds,
from one home to another home,
and nowhere that feels like mine.

Dope and Diamonds

Velvet smoke curls from cracked lips,
whispers of silk and sorrow slip through jazz-soaked
rooms,
where diamonds wink in the lamplight, cold and cruel,
but sweeter than the needle's bite, the ghost of dope's
cruel bloom.

Gilded fingers clutch the night like brittle promises,
glittering lies sewn tight in the seams of satin gloves,
each stone a frozen tear from a queen who lost her
throne,
each hit a fleeting throne built on ash and lost loves.

The diamond's gleam is sharp enough to cut through
dreams,
while dope's dull haze wraps slow like a lover's cruel
embrace,
both chained to the pulse of a city that never sleeps,
where beauty and poison wear the same painted face.

Beneath chandeliers dripping with liquid fire,
the dope dances, silent, seductive, and sly,
while diamonds chatter like laughter in crystal glasses,
both promising stars, both born to lie.

Dope and diamonds, two sisters in a twisted waltz,
one spins the mind into velvet night, soft and deep,
the other blinds the soul with cold brilliance and greed,
both treasures to cherish, both wounds that won't keep.

In smoky parlors where secrets bleed like wine,
they trade whispers of fortune and ruin alike,
and the dance goes on, under moon's pale glare,
dope and diamonds, beauty and despair.

On the edge of great

Standing right here, trembling, on the edge of great,
where the lights blur, and the crowd's roar feels like
thunder inside my chest,
the dream so close it tastes like fire on my tongue,
but the fear, oh, the fear, it holds me tighter than any
hand ever could.

A heartbeat's breath away from breaking free,
from stepping into a spotlight that promises everything
and nothing all at once,
the music hums in my veins like electricity,
but my feet feel glued to the ground,
 caught between who I was and who I'm supposed to
become.

There's a phantom voice whispering doubts in the quiet,
telling me I'm not ready, that the light will burn me,
but I see them, those souls who dared to jump,
who stumbled and rose, who danced with ghosts of their
own fears,
and they're waiting, waiting for me to take the leap.

This isn't just a stage, not just a song,
it's the crack in the world where hope spills through,
a place where dreams bleed raw and real,
and every note, every step is a heartbeat closer to
greatness.

So I stand here, breath shaky, hands clenched,
on the edge of great, where the fall is just as loud as the
flight,
where the music doesn't stop, and neither can I.

Because maybe greatness isn't about never falling,
it's about standing up when the silence screams,
about playing every note like it's your last chance,
and daring the world to catch you,
just as you're about to fly.

Chipped nail paint

The marigold sun sinks slow behind cracked window
panes,
casting long shadows on the faded walls of this old
haveli,
where stories seep from the cracked floors like
whispered secrets,
 and the scent of chai lingers, warm and bittersweet.

Fingers wrapped in bangles, clinking like distant temple
bells,
but the nailpaint peels away,
a delicate scarlet bleeding through chipped edges,
like the stubborn heart of a woman who won't be
polished smooth.

Her hands once danced in rangoli dust,
painted prayers traced in turmeric and vermilion,
now resting quietly on the threadbare cot,
speaking in silence of battles fought beneath silk sarees,
and dreams folded like old letters in the drawer.

The cracked paint is a map of moments,
mornings spent plucking jasmine from the courtyard,
evenings in crowded markets where the air hums with
monsoon promises,
and nights when the moon hid behind clouds,
and her heart chipped away, one longing at a time.

No lacquer can hide the cracks of living,
nor can the brightest polish mask the worn edges of a
soul
that has loved, lost, and kept on walking,
a slow dance between tradition and the fierce pulse of
becoming.

So here she sits, fingers bare and beautiful,
chipped nailpaint catching the last light like a secret,
reminder that even the most imperfect stories
carry their own kind of color,
deep, raw, and endlessly alive.

Brewing tea on a dull morning

The walls stay the same, familiar shadows hold their
places,
but the furniture shifts, reluctant dancers learning new
steps,
the old foldable chair folds out into a different corner,
where afternoon light falls softer, like a whispered
secret.

The worn-out bookshelf finds a new home,
cradling stories like old friends,
and I build a library in the quietest corner,
stacked dreams teetering on weathered wood,
waiting for fingers to brush their spines once again.

The cracked pot of a side table leans just so,
balancing memories I'm not ready to discard,
while the rug that once stretched beneath the door
now folds back on itself, a patchwork of faded colors,
tucked like a secret beneath my feet.

I pull curtains to catch the sunlight differently,
letting shadows play on the walls I thought I knew,
and replace a vase, not with flowers, but with empty
spaces,
because sometimes emptiness is the softest kind of
filling.

Each corner holds a story retold, a memory rearranged,
familiar faces shifting like old photographs pressed into

frames,
and in the quiet hum of this constant moving,
I find new ways to breathe beneath the same roof,
discovering that a home doesn't need walls to change,
just the courage to move, to adjust,
to make space for who I am becoming
within the places I never left.

20

They say your twenties are golden.
But mine began in silence ,
no confetti,
just cold tiles and the distant sound of neighbors waking
up
to lives fuller than mine.

No calls.
No messages lighting up my screen like they used to.
No one even pretending to remember
except the app on my phone that asked
"Want to see your memories from last year?"
No,
not really.

I ate breakfast like any other day,
except today was supposed to matter.
And it didn't.

I was supposed to feel something ,
but twenty just felt like nineteen,
with heavier bones and darker circles.

I kept checking my phone.
Like maybe love would forget it left me
and show up at the door
with a bad joke and a balloon.

But it didn't.
So I sat alone.
Said "happy birthday" to the kitchen light
as I opened the fridge
and celebrated with old leftovers
 and one single thought:

What if this is all there is?

Not parties.
Not people.
Not celebration.

Just silence.
And me.
Still here.
Still breathing.

Bread and butter

We walk side by side,
your fingers barely brushing mine,
until the lamppost rises like a question between us.
You take the left. I take the right.
And the air stretches thin with silence.
"Bread and butter," we whisper.
Like it's a spell.
Like love is a kitchen thing,
soft and spreadable,
meant to stick to the corners of a good morning.

But what if I forget to say it one day?
What if you don't say it back?
Will we quarrel like the old wives say?
Will something sharper wedge its way
into the seam of our closeness,
like a knife that's only meant to slice
but not to mend?

Because I've watched butter melt away on toast,
watched it disappear into pores and edges,
the way love sometimes seeps into habits
until it's no longer tasted, just expected.

So we say it, every time.
Even at 2 AM after a fight.
Even when the pole comes and we barely notice
until it splits us like doubt.
"Bread and butter," I call out,

and you say it too,
because buttered bread cannot be undone,
and neither can we,
if we believe in small things,
in silly charms,
in the glue between breakfast and bitterness.

Let others call it childish.
Let others walk on, separate and unbothered.
But we,
we'll keep saying it,
like it's holy.
Like it's hope.
Like it's the last defense
against a world that loves
to pull people apart.

Marry, Kiss or Kill

Marry the quiet breath between thunderstorms,
the soft echo of promises stitched in moonlight,
like a lullaby humming beneath worn curtains,
but what if the silence grows too loud,
a tidal wave drowning whispered vows in shadow?

Kiss the wildfire tangled in tangled hair,
the fevered pulse that burns through midnight's skin,
a reckless dance on shattered glass,
but what if the flames devour the map,
and all that remains is smoke and aching bones?

Kill the phantom echo of forgotten dreams,
the ghost of laughter hanging in empty rooms,
a name carved in the bark of fading trees,
but what if cutting loose tears open the wound wider,
and the bleeding never learns to cease?

Marry the steady hands that cradle cracked skies,
kiss the chaos that crashes like ocean waves,
kill the past that haunts in whispered lies.

And here I am, a fragile star caught between storms,
spinning like a leaf caught in the breath of the wind,
my heart a quiet battlefield of love and loss,
searching for the meaning in this reckless ache,
wondering if love is just a question
we're too afraid to ask out loud.

Marry, kiss, or kill,
but maybe love is the art of breaking,
of falling apart,
and still choosing to stay.

The locks of my hair

The locks of my hair curl like whispered secrets,
dancing wild and free in sunlight's golden kiss,
each spiral a story, a laugh, a sigh,
a soft rebellion wrapped around my shoulders,
tumbling like waves in a sea that's just mine.

I love how they catch the breeze,
like tiny hands reaching for the sky,
how they bounce with every step I take,
a quiet symphony of joy I wear without shame.

In mornings tangled, messy, and real,
they hold the memories of dreams and late-night talks,
the comfort of warmth, the softness of home,
a crown I never need to take off.

And when the world tries to tame,
to pull and twist what wants to be wild,
I smile, knowing these curls are my own kind of magic,
beautiful, untamed, endlessly me.

The locks of my hair ,
my forever dance, my quiet smile,
my love letter to myself
written in every twist and turn.

Marbles over Pebbles

They're down by the river again,
my cousins.
Throwing water at each other like it's a weapon and a
love language.
The sky's that hazy kind of blue,
you know, the one that smells like wet bark and guava
skin.
And I'm just here.
On the porch.
Sweating and smiling and remembering.

Because it's strange,
how loud joy used to be.
Back when we picked marbles over pebbles,
without even thinking.
Marbles were the obvious choice.
Shiny. Special.
They looked like someone captured the whole sky
and trapped it in glass.

We used to sit in the dirt, remember?
Our knees always scabbed, shirts stained with the kind
of effort you only give when you really care about
something that doesn't matter.
We made rules.
Big ones.
Drawn with chalk or scratched with sticks.
Lines we'd never cross,

until we did.
And then we laughed and made new ones.

I remember the click of them,
The way they knocked into each other like they had
something to say.
Each one had a name.
A story.
We'd win them. Lose them.
Trade them for biscuits or lies or dares.
I once gave my favorite blue one away
because a boy told me I ran like the wind.
(I didn't. I tripped on a rock right after.)

And the pebbles,
they were always there.
Just lying around.
Too dull.
Too real.
We never chose them.
They didn't sparkle.
Didn't make your chest feel like it might burst
if you won one more.

But marbles?
Those were galaxies.
Little swirls of wonder that made you believe
you were holding something sacred.
Like maybe if you held it long enough,
you'd understand the whole world.

I think we stopped playing around the same time
We stopped believing summers would last forever.
One monsoon came,
we buried them, our marbles,
under the neem tree,
in a rusted tin,
like a treasure we swore we'd come back for.
We never did.
We outgrew the dirt before we outgrew missing it.

Now I pick up pebbles sometimes,
on walks, near lakes, even in cities,
like I'm waiting for one to feel different.
To hum, to glow.
To feel like *then*.

But they never do.

And I guess that's the thing about growing up,
you stop flicking your thumb at the world
and just start carrying things instead.
Bills. Deadlines. Memories so thick they settle in your
bones.

The kids down by the river just found a frog.
They're losing their minds over it, screaming and
laughing.
And God, I hope they never forget today.
I hope they never stop picking the shiny thing,
never stop trading joy like it's the most natural currency
in the world.

I hope when they're older,
they sit on some porch like this one,
barefoot, burnt brown by the sun,
and remember the exact sound of a marble hitting
another marble
like a heartbeat, like a promise, like everything.

cut to intermission

The room emptied in slow motion, shadows folding into corners like tired memories retreating from the edges of light, while the hum of distant voices softened into silence and every glance felt like a question hanging in the thick, waiting air , a breath held too long between what was said and what was left unsaid, like the weight of footsteps paused on cracked pavement before the rain falls, the story suspended in that fragile moment where time forgets to move, and all that remains is the quiet echo of unfinished sentences and the restless pulse of everything we didn't quite say but meant anyway.

Palm reading with a deck of cards

I sat across the worn wooden table, the air thick with
incense and old paper,
while he shuffled the deck like a magician hiding secrets
between his fingers,
Kings and Queens, Jacks slipping past Diamonds and
Hearts, Spades cutting the silence like a whispered
warning,
he didn't look at me, but at the cards as if they held the
breath of my days to come,
laying them out slow, like a story unfolding in sharp
edges and soft curves,
and with each card flipped, the room grew smaller,
tighter, as if the walls leaned in to listen,
He spoke not of planets or constellations, but of empires
and loves, battles and losses,
each suit like a language, each face a promise or a curse:
The King who rules over cold ambition,
the Queen who holds the weight of broken dreams,
the Jack who slips away in shadow, the Spade digging
graves for what we leave behind,

He told me the future wasn't written in the stars tonight,
but in the way those cards trembled in his hands,
a secret map of my footsteps yet to come, of hearts I
might break, of fortunes I might lose or find,
and as the last card landed face up, silent and waiting, I
felt the chill of knowing,

that maybe, just maybe, the future is less a mystery than
a game,
and we are all just players with shuffled decks, hoping to
hold the right card at the right time.

In another universe, love

In another universe,
where the sky folds differently and stars hum lullabies
we don't know,
we might have met without the weight of waiting,
without the cracks of silence between us,
our hands would have touched like old friends,
the kind who don't need words to understand the quiet
storms beneath each other's skin,
and maybe there, love wouldn't be a question wrapped in
hesitation,
but a simple truth, like sunlight spilling through a
window on a slow morning,
where time moves gently, and the heart learns to rest
without fear,
where you and I exist in the same breath, the same
moment,
unrushed, unbroken, unfolding like the petals of a flower
that never had to hide.

camouflage

I am the map folded beneath your skin,
scars like cracked rivers carving histories no one dares to
read aloud,
a geography of violence and survival written in uneven
lines,
the body's quiet rebellion stitched into flesh that refuses
to forget.

This hair, wild, untamed,
not a flaw but a forest grown in secret places,
a tangled wilderness where the mirror's judgment gets
lost,
where shame unravels and strength root-deep,
unyielding, blooms.

You think these marks are damage, but they are armor,
a language of pain turned to power,
each rough edge a shield, each shadow a sanctuary,
camouflage worn not to hide, but to endure,
to move unseen through eyes that only see what they
want to break.

I learned to disappear beneath the weight of stares,
to fold my body into the cracks of the world,
but here, beneath this broken skin,
a fierce universe breathes and burns,
holding more than scars and hair, holding truth,
the unspoken wildness of a soul refusing to be tamed.

Symbiosis

We live like two rivers tangled beneath the earth,
each carving paths that both resist and shape the other,
sometimes flooding, sometimes drying,
carrying secrets we never dared to speak aloud,
a fragile war waged in silence,
where one cannot breathe without the other learning how
to hold its breath,
where the line between self and other blurs into
something raw and real,
something neither fully owns,
a dance of shadow and light,
of hunger and surrender,
where survival means leaning into the ache of belonging
and losing all at once.

I cling onto hope like a vine set on fire

I cling onto hope like a vine set on fire,
wrapping itself around every splintered branch of my
trembling heart,
twisting and curling, desperate and wild, even as the
flames crawl higher,
burning through leaves that once felt soft and green,
turning them to ash that drifts like ghosts in the heavy
air,
and still, the vine refuses to let go,
because letting go would mean falling into the dark,
would mean giving up on the faint pulse beneath the
roar,
that stubborn flicker of light no blaze can fully consume,
it's the fierce hunger in the bones that says even when
you're burning,
you're still alive, still reaching, still fighting for the
breath that means something beyond this fire.

spiders don't weave their webs anymore

Spiders don't weave their webs anymore,
their silk-threaded dreams frayed and forgotten like
whispered secrets in a hollow house,
each fragile strand a silver ghost, trembling against the
wind of vanished promises,
no longer spun with the patience of ancient weavers,
but dropped like shattered glass on the floor of a silent
forest,
where the air tastes thick with absence,
and shadows hang heavy like old regrets refusing to
fade.

The webs, once delicate cathedrals of capture,
now crumble like brittle lace on empty branches,
their geometry undone, like broken prayers whispered in
a language no one remembers,
and the spiders, those quiet architects of stillness and
patience,
have folded their legs beneath the weight of forgotten
songs,
vanishing like smoke from a dying fire,
leaving behind only the ache of space where hope used
to hang,
a fragile tapestry unraveling thread by thread into the
dusk.

Three reasons why it happened the way it did

First,
because silence isn't just empty space,
it's a slow poison that creeps through bones and lungs,
choking out words before they even reach your mouth,
turning every conversation into a battlefield of unspoken
war,
where every glance becomes a grenade,
and every pause is a knife twisted deep,
we learned to speak in wounds,
but the words always bled too late.

Second,
because time is a thief with dirty hands,
stealing moments while we blink,
leaving us holding the hollowed-out shells of what used
to be,
 each second a jagged shard cutting into the soft parts,
and we kept patching the cracks with lies and half-truths,
but the fractures grew,
until nothing was whole anymore,
just broken pieces we tried to fit together in the dark.

Third,
because pride is a goddamn fortress built on cracked
glass,
and we were too stubborn, too scared,
to tear down the walls and show the raw mess inside,

so we armored ourselves with silence and fury,
letting anger grow like wildfire instead of asking for
mercy,
holding tight to the hurt like it was the last thing we
owned,
forgetting that to heal,
sometimes you have to fall apart first.

And maybe,
maybe the real reason is fear,
fear of being seen,
really seen,
with all the cracks and scars and desperate, aching parts,
fear that if we drop the act,
if we stop hiding behind the noise,
we'll be left naked in the cold,
and no one will catch us.

So this is why it happened,
because sometimes love isn't enough to save us from
ourselves,
because sometimes the hardest fight
is the one inside,
where we wage war against the only person who could
ever really hold us whole.

Is it obvious how infatuated I am?

I keep pretending I don't notice the way your hand rests
on the edge of things,
coffee cups, book spines, my attention.
I tell myself it's just muscle memory,
this tilt in my body when you walk into the room,
like gravity shifts and no one else feels it but me.

You speak and I nod like I'm only half-listening,
but I'm cataloguing everything,
the way your voice dips on vowels,
the nervous scratch you make behind your ear,
how your sentences hang in the air
 long after you've moved on.

I write entire essays in my head
about what your laugh does to the atmosphere,
how it softens something in me
I didn't even know had hardened.

I sit beside you like I don't want to inch closer,
like I'm not dying to brush against the edge of your
sleeve,
like I don't imagine whole lifetimes in the space
between our knees.

You ask me how my day was
and I try to remember who I was before you asked.

I say "fine"
when what I mean is,
Say my name again like it belongs to you.

I tell myself I'm composed, that I'm cool,
that no one can tell,
but my voice betrays me in its softness,
my eyes keep tripping over your mouth,
and when you say goodbye,
I wear the echo like perfume,
hoping you catch a trace of it
on your way home.

Soulstice

It happened quietly, not like a storm,
but like dusk deciding to stay a little longer than it
should.
The kind of turning that doesn't ask permission,
just slips its hands beneath your ribs
and rearranges the furniture inside you.

I stopped marking time with clocks
and started counting the things I no longer said out loud.
The air changed before I did,
grew thicker, sweeter, like something was ripening
or rotting,
and I couldn't tell which.

My shadow stretched longer than it used to,
begging for light but curling into the dark like it knew
the dark's name.
They say solstice is the longest night,
but this felt different,
this was soulstice.
The slow ache of growing in a direction no one could
see,
the grief of shedding a skin you once called home.

I stayed still.
I let it hurt.
I listened to the wind press its cold mouth
against my shoulder blades
and I didn't flinch.

Something ancient in me,
older than memory,
younger than breath,
was waking up
and asking for nothing but space.

It's not healing exactly,
this shift.
It's the pause between breaking
and becoming.
A reckoning of softness.
A night that holds you,
but refuses to promise morning.

Limerence

It's not love, not really,
it's the way your name loops through my thoughts like a
skipping record,
the way I pause in the middle of sentences
because I think I heard your voice,
or maybe just the shape of it
pressed into the air around me.

It's the ache of almost,
of wanting so badly to be known
that I start practicing our conversations
like lines in a play that'll never be staged.
You laugh in my head more often than you do in real
life,
and in the versions I rehearse,
you always choose me.

I overread everything,
your glance becomes a lifeline,
your texts a prophecy,
your silence a kind of punishment
I think I must deserve.
I keep rewriting reality
until it resembles the kind of tenderness
I'm desperate to believe you're capable of.

It's ridiculous,
this hunger for a version of you that might not even
exist.

But you smile once,
and I'm ruined for hours.
You say my name,
and I carry it in my mouth like sugar,
melting slow and dangerous.

Limerence is a kind of madness,
a gentle hallucination,
a hopeful wound.
It's the sweetest ache,
a song you hum under your breath
even though you don't remember the words,
or if they were ever yours to begin with.

And still, I hold on,
to the echo of you,
to the dream of maybe,
to the fragile, trembling edge
of something that almost feels like love
if I close my eyes hard enough.

Mansplaining/ no access

They handed me a locked room
then asked why I wasn't inside it,
told me the code was simple,
I just had to "speak up more"
while they rearranged my sentences
to fit the shape of their comfort.

He explained the thing I built
with diagrams drawn in air,
repeating my theory
like it was his epiphany
and not the one I bled over at 3AM
in a coffee-stained notebook
he never bothered to ask about.

My voice,
a passenger seat to his microphone.
My hands,
still marked from knocking on doors
he walked through without even touching the handle.

"No access,"
they say with a smile
while tossing keys to the ones
who never had to ask for them.
I write on the walls in chalk
because they don't give me paper.
I speak in parentheses.
I lead in footnotes.

And still,
he leans across the table
to translate me to myself,
as if my language
needs his permission
to sound like the truth

My life packed in a single room apartment

Everything I own fits in the reach of my arms,
 a mattress on the floor that sags like a tired body,
 a kettle that whistles louder than any conversation I've
had this week,
 a chipped mug that once belonged to someone who
believed
 I'd grow into something better.

There's a window that faces the brick wall of another
apartment
and still, I open it every morning
like hope might slip through somehow.
The walls don't echo anymore,
they've learned the weight of my silence.

The suitcase in the corner still smells like the last city I
left behind,
and I haven't unpacked the bottom half,
because it feels easier to pretend
I'm only here for a little while.

My books sit spine-up like graves,
 dog-eared and reread,
 the only voices that know the shape of my loneliness.
I water the one plant I haven't named
because if I name it, I'll mourn it when it dies.
I keep its leaves clean, like it's my guest,

and speak to it on the days
when speaking to myself feels too honest.

There are receipts from grocery runs
where I overthink fruit
and underbuy joy,
and a playlist that skips on track seven
but I let it,
because it reminds me I'm not in control of everything.

This apartment is not a home,
but it holds my ghosts gently,
the version of me that wanted more,
the version that settled,
the one that still believes
in something soft
happening soon.

flowers filled with betrayal

I didn't know betrayal could bloom,
not until you handed me a bouquet wrapped in silence,
petals trembling like they knew what I didn't,
your fingers careful not to touch mine,
your smile soft, rehearsed,
like a closing scene with no promise of another act.

There were roses,
but their red looked like warning,
like a throat mid-scream,
I should've known better than to trust a color that burns
and pretends it's love.

You said you picked them fresh,
but they wilted the moment I held them,
as if they could feel the lie
still clinging to your hands.

The lilies smelled too sweet,
funeral sweet,
too white to trust,
a kind of peace I didn't ask for.
They looked me in the eye
and didn't blink.

I kept them on my table for a week,
watched them die like your promises did,

slow,
graceful,
quietly cruel.
I didn't throw them out.
I let them turn brown at the edges
because even rot felt like a reason
to keep something close.

You gave me flowers,
but not love.
You gave me beauty,
but not truth.
And now, every time I see a blooming thing,
I wonder what it had to lose
to look that lovely
while breaking.

I didn't know how to say it.
The kind of sorry that tastes like rust,
that sticks in your throat like paper cuts,
that would've torn both of us open
if I'd spoken it aloud.
So I bought flowers instead,
as if petals could patch the places where I failed you.

I stood in front of rows and rows of forgiveness
disguised in vases.
Picked the ones that looked the least like grief,
the ones that screamed *Look, I still care,*
even though I hadn't called.

I knew you'd see it for what it was,
an apology with roots too shallow to stay.
I knew it,
but I handed them to you anyway,
hoping the silence between us
would soften under the weight of something beautiful.

I watched your fingers hover over the ribbon
like they didn't want to be fooled again.
You said "thank you"
like you were burying something.
I nodded.
Cowardice looks a lot like stillness when you don't
move fast enough.

And when I left,
I imagined the flowers drooping by nightfall,
because even beauty knows when it's been used.
Even petals turn their faces away
·from the kind of guilt that clings too long.

I gave you flowers,
because I couldn't give you truth.
Because the damage already bloomed inside me,
and I was hoping
you wouldn't notice
the scent of goodbye
buried beneath the stems.

A home of my own

The walls stay the same, familiar shadows hold their
places,
but the furniture shifts, reluctant dancers learning new
steps,
the old foldable chair folds out into a different corner,
where afternoon light falls softer, like a whispered
secret.

The worn-out bookshelf finds a new home,
cradling stories like old friends,
and I build a library in the quietest corner,
stacked dreams teetering on weathered wood,
waiting for fingers to brush their spines once again.

The cracked pot of a side table leans just so,
balancing memories I'm not ready to discard,
while the rug that once stretched beneath the door
now folds back on itself, a patchwork of faded colors,
tucked like a secret beneath my feet.

I pull curtains to catch the sunlight differently,
letting shadows play on the walls I thought I knew,
and replace a vase, not with flowers, but with empty
spaces,
because sometimes emptiness is the softest kind of
filling.

Each corner holds a story retold, a memory rearranged,
familiar faces shifting like old photographs pressed into
frames,
and in the quiet hum of this constant moving,
I find new ways to breathe beneath the same roof,
discovering that a home doesn't need walls to change,
just the courage to move, to adjust,
to make space for who I am becoming
within the places I never left.

The Last Poem

This is the last poem I will write,
not because the words have dried,
but because my hands can no longer hold the weight
of ink and unsaid things.

Sleepless nights have carved trenches under my eyes,
and my mind is a tangle of frayed threads,
too full, too raw,
bursting at the seams with a thousand echoes.

I have spilled more than I should,
poems soaked in grief,
lines heavy with hope,
verses that trembled on the edge of breaking.

But now, the page is just a mirror,
reflecting a soul worn thin,
a heart emptied of its fire,
words fading like the last embers of a dying flame.

I am tired of chasing ghosts in syllables,
tired of wrestling with silence that screams louder
than any verse.

So here, in this final breath,
I lay down my pen, not as defeat,
but surrender to the stillness within.

Because sometimes the loudest poem
is the one left unspoken,

the one that lives
in the quiet between the lines.

This is my last poem,
not the end,
but the peace that comes
when the story finally lets go.

Acknowledgements

To the quiet moments that slipped between the rush and ache of days,
thank you for giving me breath and stillness when the world forgot to pause,
for letting my scattered thoughts take shape in soft and sacred ways,
and for showing me that art can be born without applause.

To the ones who whispered gently when my voice was worn and low,
thank you for holding space for every unfinished line,
for lighting lamps inside my chest when I had nowhere to go,
for standing with me in silence, and calling what I wrote divine.

To my father, thank you for your steady, constant care,
for standing beside me with love that never had to shout.
 Your quiet pride became the strength I didn't know was there,
and your belief in me silenced every inch of doubt.

To my mother, whose absence wraps around every breath I take,
you may be gone, but your love still holds my hand.
You gave me poetry like others give heirlooms for memory's sake,
a blessing that blooms in me, gentle and grand.

I hope you are proud of the verses I shaped with your grace,
of the way I still find you in every poem I write.
 I miss you in ways no stanza can fully trace, but your spirit lives in every metaphor, in every line of light.

To Prof. Dr. Lakshmi Muthukumar, thank you for showing me the pulse of a poetry,
for teaching me that feeling is not weakness, but a gift to hold dear.
To Mrs. Vidya Hariharan, who made each verse feel like home,
and To Dr. Seema C,
who introduced us to Anne Sexton with the tenderness of someone passing down something sacred,
thank you for opening the door to a kind of poetry that didn't ask to be pretty, only real,
because in Sexton's aching honesty, in the way she wrote like she was trying to save herself,
 I saw my own shadows reflected, and for the first time,
 I felt that even the most fractured parts of me were worthy of being written, and maybe even understood.

Thank you for introducing me to poets who echoed my silent cries,
whose words found me when I could not find myself at all.
You gave me their language, their wings, their skies,
and helped me stand tall, even when I felt small.

To my English Literature batch,
thank you for making poetry feel like rebellion,
for the laughter between lectures, the scribbles passed
like secrets,
and for reminding me that writing wasn't just a subject,
it was a way of being seen, and loved, for exactly who
we are.

To Anvita Gore, thank you for being both critic and
friend,
for offering your insight with patience, honesty, and
care.
You helped these poems bend and breathe and mend,
and I'm so grateful you were willing to be there.

To the ink that spilled when I had no voice to speak,
and the paper that waited with arms open wide,
thank you for carrying the dreams I was too tired to seek,
for being the place where my truth could hide.

And to you, dear reader, thank you for meeting me here
in this soft, fragile space,
for giving your time to hold the pages of my heart.
If these words bring even a flicker of comfort or grace,
then maybe this book was never just mine from the start.

This is for the ones who write when the world tells them
to be still,
for the ones who feel deeply, and don't walk away.
This is for those who carry stories not out of want, but
will,

and for anyone who has ever loved poetry enough to stay
and let it ignite your heart.

With all my love,
 Always.

Christina Dcosta